UNSHACKLED

REIMAGINING THE PRACTICE OF LAW

Paul Llewellyn

PAUL T. LLEWELLYN

LIONCREST
PUBLISHING

UNSHACKLED
Reimagining the Practice of Law

FIRST EDITION

ISBN   978-1-5445-3908-9 *Hardcover*
       978-1-5445-3909-6 *Paperback*
       978-1-5445-3910-2 *Ebook*
       978-1-5445-3801-3 *Audiobook*

To Charlotte and Henry.

Never settle.

CONTENTS

INTRODUCTION

Growing up in Brighton, England, Thursday evenings were the highlight of my week. That was the night that I got to sit down and watch *L.A. Law*, an American show that followed the lawyers at the fictitious law firm of McKenzie, Brackman, Chaney and Kuzak. The firm had a variety of lawyers: the partner who only cared about the bottom line, the idealistic young lawyer, the criminal lawyer, the family lawyer. In reality, very few law firms have every type of lawyer, but this was the utopia that was *L.A. Law*. Each episode allowed me to follow a case from beginning to end, often touching on several contemporary issues along the way. There were episodes about the death penalty, about racism and sexism in the law profession, and about cutting-edge legal issues involving AIDS, Big Tobacco, and pharmaceutical companies.

I was ten years old in the mid-1980s when *L.A. Law* first aired, and despite the fact that the show dealt with heavy issues, it glamorized the practice of law in my eyes. I learned that law could be a noble profession, where lawyers worked with passion and conviction to do the best they could for their clients. I was exposed to a lot of American shows, from *The A-Team* to *Knight Rider* to *Baywatch*. But it was *L.A. Law* that really captured my imagination.

The show had such an influence on me that I announced to my mother I wanted to grow up to be a litigator in Los Angeles. Not only that, but I also informed her that I was changing my name to "Paul Sifuentes" after Victor Sifuentes, the character portrayed by Jimmy Smits on the show. He was my favorite character not only because he was a fantastic lawyer, but also because he had a strong moral compass and an unshakable sense of justice. I wanted to lead that life. I wanted to dispense justice in a California courtroom and then step outside and marvel at the towering skyscrapers and the dazzling lights. All I knew of California was what I had learned from *L.A. Law* and *Baywatch*, but I knew that it was the place I wanted to be.

Now, years later, I am living that life. I am a litigator and founding partner of a successful firm in California. Happily, I found out that the profession of law is just as exciting as that ten-year-old back in England thought it would be. In fact, real courtrooms often come with more drama than the ones you see on television. There is no greater rush than trying a case and then waiting for a jury to announce its verdict. Anything can happen. And finding out that a jury has decided in favor of your client reaps an unimaginable sense of pride and satisfaction at a job well done. I've been fortunate to represent truly remarkable individuals and companies, and knowing that I'm helping them successfully navigate the legal system is, in many ways, its own reward.

But while it might be as *exciting*, it isn't always as glamorous or fulfilling as it seemed on TV. For a variety of reasons (many of which I'll discuss in this book), the profession is filled with dissatisfaction on the part of everyone involved, whether that's lawyers and judges or clients and the public at large.

A 2016 study revealed that approximately 20 percent of all lawyers suffer from alcohol dependencies. Another noteworthy finding in this study: 84.1 percent of the attorneys had consumed alcohol in the prior year, compared to 69.5 percent of adults in the general population.[1] Others in the profession simply aren't happy: they hate their jobs or don't feel appreciated or valued. Often, their clients aren't happy either. In many ways, the system is broken. We've gone from a fictional utopia to a sorry state of affairs.

The good news is that there are a lot of incredibly smart, dedicated people in the legal field. Most people enter the profession with a sincere desire to serve the public. But somehow, somewhere along the way, that desire gets lost. Why does this happen? How can we do better as a profession? And in turn, how can we restore the trust and confidence of both clients and the public in our profession?

In this book, I'll lay out a path toward a healthier, more sustainable legal profession (spoiler alert: it happens to look a lot like my own firm, Lewis & Llewellyn). I'm not trying to suggest that I know it all, but I do know that one of the great things about being a lawyer is that you never stop learning. Lewis & Llewellyn isn't perfect, and like every other law firm, we can always do better. We are constantly trying to improve, to be a better firm today than we were yesterday. And based on my experience along four different career paths and both sides of the Atlantic,

I have a unique perspective on what we can all do to create a more humane and human-centered profession.

I began my legal career as a law student at Oxford University. From that vantage point, the path to California wasn't at all apparent, so I resigned myself to becoming the English equivalent of a trial lawyer—a barrister. But then, at the conclusion of my first year, I learned of a program in Los Angeles that allowed Oxford law graduates to serve as law clerks for a prestigious firm. It was a dream opportunity. Since there was no internet at the time, I ended up going to the library and researching as much as I could about the firm and its lawyers.

Just a few weeks after my name was put forward, the founding partners at this firm happened to be coming to Oxford, so they invited me to the house they had rented to interview me for the position. They were incredibly nice; however, I was also hugely intimidated by their experience. Somehow, I managed to impress, and they offered me the position. In that moment, my *L.A. Law* dream began to look a lot more real.

Once in California, I eventually found my way to Pacific Palisades, an ocean-side enclave just north of Santa Monica. I'd never heard of the place, so I asked one of my new colleagues if it was a nice neighborhood and was assured it was pretty good. I soon found out it was actually home to the rich and famous. At that point, I was far from either. For starters, I didn't even have a car, which is essential in LA, where practical public transportation is very limited and traffic is so bad that it is measured in hours and minutes, rather than miles. With no credit history, I ended up having to spend way too much money leasing a broken-down, fifteen-year-old Volvo that sounded more like a tank than an automobile. Clearly, life in Los Angeles wasn't going to be as glamorous as I thought it would be.

But all of that hassle and uncertainty melted away every time I stepped inside the firm. There, I was immersed in some of the most noteworthy cases of the time, including one brought by the Marlboro Man's widow. Tragically, the actor who played the Marlboro Man had died of lung cancer after years of smoking while filming commercials for the brand. Another case involved workers at a nuclear power plant who had come down with a rare form of cancer. Before I arrived there, the firm had also defended Suzuki from allegations that the Suzuki Samurai flipped over too easily. These were all big-time cases that made headlines locally and nationally. Being right in the middle of it, working on great cases with outstanding colleagues, was a once-in-a-lifetime experience.

Soon my nine-month appointment was up, and I had to head back home. I knew I wanted to practice law in California, but I didn't see how I could do so in the short term.

Back in England, I started on my mandatory vocational training to become a barrister, known as "bar school." This one-year course consisted of hands-on practical training, where I learned English civil procedure, cross-examination, negotiation, and more. The next hurdle to becoming a barrister in England is to get what's called a pupillage, a mandatory one-year apprenticeship. Effectively, I became a trainee barrister with no guarantee that I would get taken on by chambers (a group of lawyers practicing together, kind of like an American firm) at the end. In this position, I would draft documents and often make cup after cup of tea for my pupil master. It was the lowest position, but I was glad to have joined a wonderful set of chambers in Temple, London. At the end of it, I was fortunate enough to be given a tenancy, which is something like tenure for teachers. If you have a tenancy, you are at that chambers for life—unless you royally fuck up.

Despite my comfortable position and excellent colleagues, the California itch continued to nag at me. English courtrooms just didn't have the same level of drama as a Los Angeles courtroom. California has the largest legal system in the nation. The Stanley Mosk Courthouse in LA is eight stories with one hundred courtrooms and a press area on every floor. English magistrates' courts tend not to have press areas at all.

So when the firm I had been with in Los Angeles called me to offer me a position as an associate, I was in a dilemma. On one hand, I was already quite successful, having found a position at a chambers and then gotten a tenancy. I had accomplished what every law student at Oxford hoped to achieve, so why should I give it up to go chasing a dream? Then again, I might never have an opportunity like this again. It was a difficult decision, but the fact that I'm writing this book from California tells you exactly what I did.

As I packed for my move to Los Angeles, I imagined myself as the stereotypical immigrant who arrives in America with nothing but one suitcase, ready to follow the American dream. When I tell this story to my colleagues today, they say, "Yes, you arrived with nothing but one suitcase...*and* your Oxford law degree."

Fair point.

That said, it was not immediately smooth sailing for me. My

first hurdle was the California bar exam. Passing that exam was tougher than getting a degree from Oxford, mostly because I had only eight weeks to learn what American law students learn in three years. Even though the US legal system is based on the English system, they are still fundamentally different. It didn't help matters that the California bar was tough, with only a typical pass rate of around 40 percent—less for international students. I studied fifteen hours a day for those eight weeks; nevertheless, a real chance that I would fail remained, which put my position at the firm in jeopardy.

Fortunately, I passed. That was one of the proudest days of my life. I celebrated that night in Pacific Palisades with Kentucky Fried Chicken and a glass of chardonnay. Twenty-one years have passed since that California bar exam. I still feel the same buzz I felt as a newly minted US attorney each time I walk into a California courtroom. But while the excitement remains, I've now seen some of the starker and more troubling realities of the legal world.

I've watched talented lawyers burn out or leave the profession for other endeavors. I've seen judges and clients become disillusioned by unnecessary hurdles and barriers, especially financial ones. And I've come to believe that not only that we can all do better, but also that we have an ethical imperative to do so. Does that belief make this book a manifesto? Perhaps somewhat. If nothing else, I hope it prompts real examination and discussion about the profession and how we can improve it.

Even though I have broad experience when it comes to practicing law, I, of course, don't claim to know it all or have a solution for every problem. Full disclosure: I am coming at these issues from a litigator's point of view, and even though we like to joke that we're the only "true" attorneys, I understand that my perspective is limited. What I am hoping to provide is a path forward, a way to improve the profession and help attorneys who are struggling in a world that is changing fast, and not always for the better.

The practice of law is troubled by issues of inequality that are not easily solved. Yet resolving these problems is essential to creating the kind of profession that I want to see. I won't pretend that I know how to solve the equity problem in law, particularly as that problem relates to diversity and hiring, but I will say that working toward such a solution is crucial to rebuilding a field that should be able to pride itself on fairness and objectivity.

I'm also not going to provide a quick fix that will reform the legal industry overnight. Nor is this book going to instantly make your professional and personal life more rewarding. I'm not going to unpack the entire American legal system, nor am I going to take down Biglaw or Big Business. There are dozens of important issues that I won't be able to cover in the depth that they deserve.

But I will lay out a practical plan that, based on my experience, can improve the lives of lawyers, no matter their background. I'll explore how and why the legal profession has gone astray and what we can all do to help get it back. I believe strongly that there is no more noble profession than the field of law. Every day, lawyers have the opportunity to help clients, often during the lowest point in their lives and sometimes when their very existence is on the line. We have been endowed with both tremendous responsibility and the opportunity to do real good. Working together, we can make the legal system a place that is fair and rewarding for all.

Chapter 1

"YOU CAN'T HANDLE THE TRUTH": WHY REAL LAWYERS ARE FALLING SHORT OF POP CULTURE COUNTERPARTS

"I was recently watching a television debate in which a medical doctor was slamming lawyers as a drain on society. I would like to remind the doctor that while his professional ancestors were putting leeches on George Washington to bleed him, my ancestors were writing the declaration of independence and the United States constitution."

—JOSEPH JAMAIL, JR.

The pop culture landscape has an enormous influence on how people view the legal profession today. As I mentioned in the introduction, *L.A. Law* inspired me to pursue a legal career. Undoubtedly, many more young people have likely been inspired by the likes of *A Few Good Men*'s Joanne Galloway and Daniel

Kaffee, *Law & Order*'s Jack McCoy or the characters of *Suits*, *The Practice*, or *Ally McBeal*. Some of our most beloved television and film characters are lawyers, and viewers delight in tuning in and watching them exact justice with grace and courtroom flair. Our culture is equally fascinated with court-based reality shows, beginning with *The People's Court* back in 1981 and culminating in the 2020 announcement that Judge Judy was the highest paid woman on television (at the time, she was making $47 million a year, or about $900,000 per episode).[2]

I'd wager that the appeal of these types of shows is the tidy way they depict the dispensing of justice: within each episode, a verdict is served, a right is wronged, and more times than not, the good guy comes out on top. I think most of us want to believe that's how the world—and the legal system—works in real life.

And yet, if you bring up the legal profession at a cocktail party or family gathering, you are more likely to be met with rolled eyes or looks of disgust than you are any sense of admiration or appreciation. The legal profession is one of the least trusted in modern society. According to a Gallup poll, only 19 percent of Americans have a very high or high opinion of the honesty and ethical standards of lawyers.[3] That puts us only slightly ahead of politicians and used car salesmen. And with all apologies to people in both professions, that is not the company I want to keep when it comes to my career and vocation.

Too many Americans view lawyers as greedy and dishonest—the complete opposite of the legal protagonists that dominate our entertainment. Why the disconnect? How can the legal profession be so admired in prime time and also so reviled in the real world? What went wrong? And more importantly, what can be done to rehabilitate the image of the legal field in the mind of the public?

CASE STUDY: THE MCDONALD'S LAWSUIT

Public perception of lawyers has never been lower. Some of that vitriol is probably deserved. But a lot of it is also the result of misperceptions repeated and engrained until they become a kind of pseudo-reality presented as fact. A famous and telling example of how the negative perception of the legal field has been erroneously created is the often-cited McDonald's coffee lawsuit from the early 1990s.

Chances are, you have heard about this case somewhere. It gets trotted out again and again as an example of a ridiculous lawsuit and lawyers who went too far. It's often seen as a benchmark for how crazy and greedy both lawyers and their clients can be. In the common retelling of this particular case, a woman sued McDonald's for millions of dollars because she spilled a cup of their coffee onto her lap while she was driving. Feigning tremendous distress, she then sought to squeeze every last penny she could out of the fast-food giant.

If that were the truth of the matter, then the criticism would be fair. But let's take a moment and look at the realities of the case.[4] Stella Liebeck, seventy-nine years old, was sitting in the passenger seat of her grandson's car having purchased a cup of McDonald's coffee. As the car stopped, she tried to hold the cup between her knees while removing the lid. The cup tipped over, pouring scalding coffee onto her. She received third-degree burns over 16 percent of her body, requiring hospitalization for eight days and numerous follow-up procedures.

It was reported that Ms. Liebeck offered to settle with McDonald's for $20,000, but McDonald's refused, reportedly offering her $800 before she filed suit. At trial the jury awarded Ms. Liebeck $200,000 in compensatory damages—reduced to $160,000 because the jury found her 20 percent at fault. It also awarded her $2.7 million in punitive damages, which the trial judge reduced to $480,000.

According to Ms. Liebeck's attorney, the jury heard that at the time, McDonald's sold coffee at 180 to 190 degrees Fahrenheit, which at that temperature causes third-degree burns in two to seven seconds. In the decade before this incident McDonald's had received seven hundred reports of people burning themselves from coffee including to their genital area, inner thighs, and buttocks.

However, McDonald's never provided its customers with a warning about how hot they served their coffee. Ms. Liebeck's treating physician testified that her injury was one of the worst scald burns he had ever seen.

Unfortunately, the McDonald's coffee lawsuit became synonymous with the excesses of litigation, and the actual details of the case were largely lost to history. Instead, the case took on a multifaceted life of its own, appearing on late-night TV monologues and as justification for proposed legislation capping damages or limiting the scope of other lawsuits. Along the way, litigators—and lawyers in general—took a big hit in the court of public opinion. While there are many problems with our justice system, the McDonald's hot coffee case is not one of them. A lot of the poor public perception of lawyers can be traced to unfair media coverage and exaggerated stories like this McDonald's example. But that's not the only reason that we have a public image problem. Sometimes the realities of the profession work against us as well.

DOLLARS AND SENSE

On most fictional TV court dramas, a seemingly endless stream of clients walks through a law firm's doors and into their well-decorated waiting rooms and offices. In fact, I can't think of a single television show or movie in which reputable lawyers are out hustling for clients or engaging in conversations around the conference room table about marketing budgets, associate recruitment and retention, or whether the firm has enough business to make their bottom line.

The fact is that all law firms are ultimately businesses: we have to earn enough money to pay associates and other staff and keep the lights on. To attract the best talent, we also have to be able to justify competitive salaries and bonuses. The question remains how best to achieve those needs while also serving our clients.

In 2020, the one hundred biggest global law firms exceeded $128 billion in combined revenues. That's on par with the GDP of countries like Morocco, Angola, and Slovakia—and that's just the one hundred biggest firms.[5] Meanwhile, equity partners at America's top one hundred firms are reported to net, on average, about $2.5 million annually, with the rainmaking partners bringing in considerably more than that.[6] The top ten most profitable firms all report profits per equity partner of over $5 million per year.[7]

Now, I am not begrudging anyone who makes that much money practicing law. Those salaries are the nature of the market. The point that I'm making here is that these law firms are huge, moneymaking machines. That much money and influence brings along with it some very justifiable scrutiny.

These large fees not only create a poor public perception, but they also make hiring a lawyer incredibly expensive—and prohibitively so for some of the individuals most in need of representation. Is that morally defensible?

We should also be asking hard questions about who, if anyone, is justified in charging these high billable rates. Is it appropriate, for instance, to pay all junior associates equally? What about someone just entering the profession and with no substantive experience trying or winning cases, or even appearing in court? Many large firms pay their new hires astronomical salaries, despite their lack of experience or time in a courtroom.

This situation stands in stark contrast to my experience as a junior barrister in England. As a twenty-three-year-old criminal prosecutor working cases, I would generally be paid about £35 (approximately $45) for an appearance. The problem was, that in order to get to court, I'd have to pay the peak train fares, which were often more than I'd make that day. There were many days as a junior barrister that I actually lost money for the privilege of being a lawyer. It wasn't good for my wallet, but the experience of going to court day in and day out was incredibly valuable. I got to experience the thrill of the courtroom and to better learn my profession in doing so. Contrast that with the way litigation unfolds in the United States, and especially California. Many attorneys have been practicing for years and have never even been inside the courtroom. However, their billing rates continue to increase.

The reality of this cost-benefit analysis leads to distrust and anger among existing and would-be clients. Many people believe lawyers are looking to profit off of their misfortunes, which is one reason why they deem the experience of dealing with an attorney an unpleasant one. These individuals aren't necessarily frustrated because their lawyers are not serving them well or not dedicated to doing a good job, but rather both because they resent having to hire an attorney in the first place and they feel justice isn't being served.

This is just another reality of the profession that serves to frustrate the public. Being a lawyer requires years of training and specialized education, so high fees will always be part of the system. When people spend money on lawyers, however, they often don't have much to show for it in the end. Unlike a vacation or a house, there is no tangible result; nor is there any guarantee of a return on investment. Clients don't often see the amount of work that goes into a case, and, as a result, they can begin to resent their lawyer. Television and movies have trained them to believe that legal disputes can be resolved on the scale of hours or weeks, and these unrealistic expectations can lead to frustration and hostility. When litigation drags on for months and then years, it can be hard for clients to shake the notion that something is going wrong. Compounding the problem is the fact that television has also convinced them that their case will result in justice being done. But the reality of the situation is often far more complex. In fact, I think justice and the law are perhaps best considered as two separate concepts.

When it comes to the realities of legal cases, clients are often forced to do a cost-benefit analysis. You can be one hundred percent in the right and still have nowhere to go from a legal standpoint. A client might truthfully say, "I'm being sued, but I did nothing wrong," and yet end up with a huge legal bill even if they win their case. It could be the case that such a client would actually save money by falsely conceding liability and agreeing to a settlement, rather than fighting to ensure that the "truth" prevails. Should they spend more money to clear their name and reputation, knowing that it might take years and tens or even hundreds of thousands of dollars, not to mention all of the anxiety and uncertainty along the way?

There are similar problems facing plaintiffs. One of Lewis & Llewellyn's dedicated missions is representing survivors of sexual abuse in civil lawsuits against perpetrators of abuse and institutions that enable it. As civil claims, as opposed to criminal prosecutions, the only remedy generally available to a plaintiff is financial restitution. They can have the strongest and most worthwhile case in the world, but if their abuser doesn't have any real assets, they won't end up receiving any restitution. One of the hardest parts of my job is telling these clients or potential clients that it's not worth pursuing a civil lawsuit because their abuser has no money. Pursuing that kind of case just makes no economic sense, and hearing that is an understandably bitter pill for these survivors. It's also a perennial frustration of mine as I seek to provide the best representation possible for my clients.

The practice of law is complex and full of trade-offs, and this reality can be a very unwelcome surprise to people who have an entirely different impression of what the legal field actually is.

POOR CUSTOMER SERVICE

It's true that the realities of the legal profession work to hurt public perception, but sometimes it's the lawyers themselves who are to blame for our bad reputation. All too often, clients deal with inattentive or incompetent lawyers. Moreover, the stereotypical unscrupulous lawyer may not exist in the numbers that some of the public assumes, but that doesn't mean that they don't exist at all.

Some lawyers are more interested in their personal gain than what's best for the client. They might bring lawsuits solely in hopes of securing a large settlement and without any consideration for whether or not that settlement is even warranted. Under American law, you generally don't have to pay the opposing side's lawyer's fees if you lose, and some lawyers take advantage of that fact, filing frivolous suits they know they'll never win. (This contrasts with the English rule, where the default is that the loser must pay the other side's legal fees.) When this is combined with the low cost for filing a lawsuit— just $435 in California—it's fairly easy for an unscrupulous lawyer to operate.

On the other hand, fee arrangements such as one in which a lawyer takes a percentage of a prospective settlement or judgment as payment—known as a contingency fee—can help ensure that meritorious cases get their day in court. It's a good system because the goals of the lawyer and the client are completely aligned. The more the client gets, the more the attorney gets. Conversely, if a client has brought an unwinnable case, that person's lawyer will suffer financially as well.

It also enables meritorious cases, i.e. where liability is strong and damages are substantial, to see the light of day. Right now, many worthwhile—and winnable—cases could not be pursued because the plaintiff simply could not afford the fees. With the contingency system, because lawyers will get a stake of the recovery, they will be more likely to pick up the case. There is even a burgeoning litigation funding industry where litigation funding companies will effectively invest in a lawsuit in exchange for a return on its investment in the event of a recovery. This can provide much-needed cash flow to law firms and again enables meritorious cases to see the light of day. Such fee arrangements—such as contingency fees or litigation funding—ensure that the best cases get the attention that they deserve. Of course, "best cases" is not a perfect concept. If the defendant has no money to pay a judgment or settlement it will be hard to convince any lawyer—even on a contingency—to take the case. This, in part, is why I said earlier that law and justice are separate concepts.

There's a fine balance that must be met when creating a just legal system. While access to justice is critical, if the barriers are too low, then there is a danger of predatory lawyers becoming far more common. Such unscrupulous lawyers undoubtedly hurt the reputation of the entire field.

THE PROBLEM OF MORALE

With so much negativity aimed at lawyers, is it any wonder that the actual job of being an attorney is not seen as satisfying? This profession teaches that terrible things happen to good people for no reason. The pressures can be immense and the hours long. The same realities of the profession that turn off the public can also work to erode the morale of even the most idealistic among us.

The toll of all of these pressures can be seen in the results of a recent mental health survey conducted by ALM, an information, data, and content company specializing in the world of law. That inquiry found that approximately 32 percent of more than 3,800 respondents felt that they were depressed, while 64 percent reported experiencing anxiety. It also found disturbing evidence of suicide within the profession. Approximately 10 percent of lawyers surveyed indicated that they had an alcohol problem; about 3 percent felt that they had a drug problem (overall, 7 percent of Americans say they have an alcohol problem; fewer than 1 percent say they have a drug problem).[8] Since these numbers are self-reported, the true toll of alcohol and drug dependency on the legal profession is almost certainly far higher.

Alcohol abuse has become such a common problem among lawyers that California now requires mandatory continuing education addressing substance abuse. However, we've barely begun to understand what a significant toll all of these problems—alcohol, drugs, depression, anxiety—add to an already pressure-filled profession. The Dave Nee Foundation in New York, a think tank for the study of lawyer depression, ranks American lawyers fifth occupationally in the incidence of suicide. According to the Nee Foundation, lawyers are the most frequently depressed occupational group in the United States and are 3.6 times more likely to suffer from depression than nonlawyers.[9] The very nature of the legal world requires us to take on our client's biggest problems, and unless lawyers find a healthy way to cope with the stress, they are bound for burn out, or, in the most extreme cases, even attempt suicide.

This already precarious situation was made worse by COVID-19. There used to be a much clearer dividing line between work life and home life, but since so many people have been working from home, it seems as if the problems associated with the job never leave them. There's no space to decompress, no place safe from the pressures of the office.

At the same time, the positive aspects of the office, such as being able to connect with or support colleagues, have been largely absent for many of us. Personally, I am a huge proponent of in-person experiences. Throughout my career, I've relied upon the commiseration and decompression that happens after a long day of court, when all the barristers congregate at a nearby pub and share war stories from the day. As a junior attorney, I benefited highly from senior associates and partners who were willing to check in and talk through a problem or ask my advice on a particular aspect of a case. Often, these were just brief hallway conversations that developed organically and in the moment. Even the best planned Zoom call can't replace that kind of interaction. Let's face it—most of us probably wouldn't care if we never had to do another Zoom again.

So much more can be done to support lawyers in their time of struggles, but it will require effort. We expect lawyers to be fulfilled, to be happy to be servicing clients well. But it's hard to do without the proper support for ourselves.

THE BRIGHT SIDE

While it's true that the public's perception of the legal profession is quite negative, there are some positive aspects we can identify as we try to find ways to improve the profession as a whole.

In the same way that many Americans feel positively about fictional legal heroes, it's also true that most Americans tend to be satisfied with their own personal lawyers. People tend to value their attorneys and rely on them—sometimes with their very lives. From closing on a house, to helping with estate matters or an ugly divorce, to providing much-needed counsel after a DUI or felony indictment, lawyers consistently help their clients navigate the byzantine and often intimidating legal system. What remains to be seen is why that valuable assistance, which is readily acknowledged by individual clients, doesn't translate into the larger (not to mention stereotypical and more reductive) image we often have, both in the media and popular perception.

The truth of the matter is that there are a lot of great people practicing law today. They are hardworking and dedicated, honest and principled. But it can often feel as if no one is lining up to sing our praises, especially for a national audience. Thankfully, there are places where you can hear positive stories about the legal profession and where the extraordinary lawyers of our time are highlighted. One of my favorites is the *The Game Changing Attorney* podcast hosted by Michael Mogill. Each week he interviews a prominent leader in the legal industry. Many of his guests are the best of the best, and it's inspiring to hear the stories of why they became lawyers and their attitude toward the profession and the current culture. Attend a national legal conference such as The Game Changers Summit, and you'll undoubtedly hear all kinds of inspiring stories from dedicated, selfless individuals who have dedicated themselves to the practice of law.

It's a positive and reassuring sign that this reality is so far removed from the stereotypes. However, we must do more to bridge that gap with the public. What can we do to once again win the public's trust in us? Working to rebuild the public image of lawyers will lead to increased lawyer satisfaction as well as increased client satisfaction. And ultimately that leads to increased public satisfaction as well.

We don't have to accept the status quo and just say, "this sucks." The whole point of this book is to re-imagine the field of law and to consider another, better way, a way that works for clients, but that works for us as well.

Most lawyers today entered the profession because they wanted to emulate the likes of Jack McCoy, Atticus Finch, or in my case, Victor Sifuentes. They have altruistic tendencies and want to do good. We need to find the best way to let them be a good guy, even if the system seems bad. And then we need to figure out how to launch our own PR campaign to rehabilitate our image in the public eye.

I joke that I would love to see "Love Your Lawyer Day" become a national holiday. I've yet to receive a card or a gift acknowledging the day, but I also haven't given up hope. While it may sound idealistic, I nevertheless believe that the public wants to root for us. We just need to give them the opportunity. And the good news is that it won't take all that much: by implementing just a few of the correctives I outline in this book, we can increase trust and raise our standing with the public.

CHAPTER 2

THE CORPORATIZATION OF LAW

"There is evidence that young men in the big law firms, although they still work harder than most of their clients, do not glory in putting in night work and weekend hours as they once did."

—DAVID RIESMAN

So much of the structure and climate of Biglaw is owed to a man most Americans have never heard of.

At the turn of the last century, Paul Drennan Cravath, a descendant of a Pennsylvania Quaker farming family, joined the law firm of Blatchford, Seward & Griswold, a prestigious Manhattan firm that specialized in the fastest growing industries of the day: steel, railroads, and emerging electrical and automobile companies. Cravath quickly made a name for himself as an attorney who could navigate the complicated world of these new industries and the nuanced legal cases they sparked.

But what really defined his legacy is what has become known as the *Cravath System*. Simply put, this eponymously named organizational strategy became the blueprint for growing big law firms. Cravath recruited almost exclusively at Ivy League schools and expected all of his job applicants to have graduated with honors and a pedigree that included time spent editing their institution's law review. He established the lockstep compensation system, in which all associates were paid the same salary based on years served. Those associates not deemed partner material were dismissed, and partners were almost always chosen from within the firm.

This model created an easily scalable approach to growing any law firm, and it wasn't long before some of the nation's leading firms employed a hundred attorneys. Although the term "Biglaw" is prone to some variance in usage, the most commonly accepted definitions would include working in a large firm, which demands long hours, and which tends to represent large corporations rather than individuals.

Today, Biglaw firms may have thousands of paid lawyers on their staff, most of whom are focused on a particular type of law. In the spirit of Paul Cravath, they tend to fastidiously match each other on salaries and compete for the top students at the most prestigious universities. They primarily represent Fortune 500 companies, handling business litigation, mergers and acquisitions, healthcare, tax, and employment law.

Say "Biglaw" to most lawyers, and they'll know exactly which law firms you are referring to. Most often, the term does not engender a warm and fuzzy feeling. And yet, too often, Biglaw is viewed as the pinnacle of the profession: a prestigious goal that should be sought by all the best law students. Along the way, it has become idealized for its salary and cultural cache, while realities such as grueling hours and inhospitable working environments get swept under the rug.

Don't get me wrong: I'm not here to trash Biglaw or to spend this chapter explaining why Biglaw and the corporatization of the legal profession is terrible. But I do think that it's important and necessary to consider the ways that Biglaw has negatively affected members of the legal profession and, perhaps more importantly, their clients as well.

One reason the culture of Biglaw is so enmeshed in our profession is because it pervades so much of the legal world, beginning with law school. Typically, the hiring process begins with top law students who are invited to become summer associates after their first or second year of schooling. I jokingly describe this so-called internship as a paid opportunity to attend cooking classes, dine at fine restaurants, and attend wine tastings. That's an exaggeration, of course, but the reality of a summer associate-ship is that the eight-week program places a lot more emphasis on social events than it does the practice of law. In the end, being a summer associate bears no relation whatsoever to what it's like to be an associate at the law firm. As a result, the summer associates get a Utopian view of what life is like at the firm.

At the end of the eight weeks, almost every summer associate is made an offer from a Biglaw firm. For those who accept that offer, their entire career path has been plotted before they've even graduated. In other words, they're now speeding along a trajectory without having any idea what kind of a ride they're truly in for.

All the major law schools also offer on-campus interviews (OCI) with large firms. As a prospective associate, you might meet with fifteen to twenty firms. Perhaps not surprisingly, some humorous and even shocking stories come out of this tradition. One of my colleagues once told me that he sat down for an OCI with the partner of a prestigious firm, who wanted to know why my colleague wanted to work for them. *I have no idea,* my colleague admitted. *You big firms all seem the same to me. What do you think sets you apart?*

I still can't decide if my colleague's tack there was brave or just ballsy. But he had a legitimate point: every law firm says they do the best work and win the most cases; that they privilege their clients and the workplace experience of even the most junior associate. After a while, they can begin to seem like carbon copies of each other. What set my colleague apart was his willingness to say that out loud.

And the partner from the firm who was interviewing him must have known my colleague was right. The partner told my colleague he found his candor refreshing and eventually offered him a job with the firm. He also confessed that he was about to leave the firm himself.

What both my colleague and that partner realized was just how difficult it is for giant firms to set themselves apart. One thing they all have in common is that their associates are working for two or three usually dead guys who established the firm and are now long gone, leaving the rest of us to toil away in the name of their legacy.

In my time as a lawyer, I've heard way too many nightmare stories about the partner who knew about a hefty assignment for a month but only bothered to assign it to a junior associate at 6:00 p.m. on Friday and demanded it be completed by the start of the workday on Monday. Or the disgruntled partner who resorted to temper tantrums whenever he didn't get his way, sometimes resorting to physical violence and throwing staplers or binders at new associates. I'll talk more about the importance of a productive firm culture in Chapter Five. But for now, it's worth noting that even the most generic Biglaw firm can—and often does—foster its own distinct reputation.

I recently reviewed a Biglaw website where the firm proudly announced it was "Biglaw Redefined." Accompanying this bold statement was a video, set to inspiring music, where the firm announced a "collaborative culture," "meaningful insight," "on-the-ground decisions," and "empowered attorneys." Truly groundbreaking stuff. No doubt a marketing consultant was paid hundreds of thousands of dollars to come up with this nonsense. If this really is "Biglaw redefined," it doesn't bode well for the future of such firms.

By way of full disclosure I should also say that I spent six very rewarding years working in Biglaw, and I'm a better attorney because of the experience. We also work closely with Biglaw attorneys at my current firm, coordinating on cases, and have had some wonderful experiences. However, it's also true that Biglaw often promotes a world in which personal connections between lawyers and clients are jettisoned in favor of profits and rankings. No matter how large or small, every firm should be focused on the value they provide to customers and clients and the excellence of service they provide. We can make money and still provide a quality human connection, rather than creating an anonymous experience concerned only with billable hours and profits.

THE PROBLEM WITH PROFITS

As I said in Chapter One, I fully accept that law firms are businesses. We all have expenses to pay, and we all deserve to be compensated fairly. We can't do either without charging fees and making money.

However, as law firms have become more like corporations, the emphasis on profits has grown to unhealthy levels. This emphasis is even reflected in the way that law firms are commonly ranked. Most aggregating sites take several factors into consideration; however, profitability is often deemed one of the most important. This obsession with profitability per partner isn't healthy, and it neglects vital benchmarks, including both employee and client satisfaction.

Meanwhile, firms dedicate undue amounts of money to the quality of their artwork, the lavishness of their reception areas, and their extravagant summer associate boondoggles—all to prove they are the most prestigious firm. And that doesn't even take into account their emphasis on matching or beating the highest salaries and bonuses in the industry!

All of the top firms watch one another's pay scales with hawk-like intensity. As a result, even yearly increases are pretty standard industry-wide. A starting salary at a Biglaw firm is typically around $215,000. Each year, you'll get an automatic pay increase. By the time you reach the giddy heights of practicing law for eight years, you can expect to be making a base salary of about $425,000. That doesn't take into account bonuses, which can easily raise that figure to a half-million dollars.

For lawyers just out of law school, bigger salaries are often attractive due to the large amount of student loan debt. As a result, students from top schools sometimes feel forced by their financial situation to take a job with Biglaw that may not suit their personality or match their ultimate career goals. That's not the ideal situation for high job satisfaction. To make matters worse, certain industry websites fuel that fire by providing breaking news on the latest bonuses offered by firms.

This obsession with money creates a frenzy and feeds into the perception that lawyers are greedy and motivated only by the bottom line. Among lawyers themselves, talk of starting salaries and annual bonuses often eclipses conversations about fulfilling cases or supportive work environments. Meanwhile, the firms themselves—whether for prestige or to attract the best talent— become so obsessed with the race to have the highest salaries and bonuses that they lose sight of any negative impact that race might have on clients.

This emphasis on financials only serves to reinforce the idea that lawyers themselves are fungible, a mere commodity to be maximized. The human beings behind the impressive numbers are rarely considered—and neither are their clients. As a result, loyalty and commitment take a back seat, and many lawyers are always hunting for their next profitable opportunity without any concern for longevity or continuity.

Firms, meanwhile, create toxic work environments where senior associates are forced to vie for sometimes just a handful of partner opportunities. Most will never make it. Meanwhile, pressures grow as they find themselves saddled with mortgages and hefty tuition payments for their kids. As these lawyers age, it becomes less feasible they'll ever secure their own roster of clients or set out to launch their own firms. The financial commitments are just too large to consider taking risks, and these attorneys soon find themselves stuck in a lucrative but unsatisfying position.

If, instead, firms were more interested in cases won and job satisfaction for their employees, they might find that they are actually building more value in the long run. If, for instance, these firms embraced a true apprenticeship approach to training and developing new associates, they might reduce their profits in the short term but soon find that they have more clients and a better reputation in the long run. Happier clients and happier lawyers can only create a better legal system overall.

LIMITED OPPORTUNITIES

With a name like Biglaw, you'd expect these corporate firms to have the greatest opportunities for new lawyers, but that isn't necessarily the case. Young, idealistic lawyers join Biglaw with the hope of doing important work, or at least seeing the inside of a courtroom. The reality is often just the opposite.

Most new associates at a Biglaw firm won't get within twenty miles of a courthouse. They rarely have the opportunity to prepare important briefs. Instead, they find themselves swamped with soul-crushing and menial tasks, such as clicking through reams of electronic files for hours at a time or sifting through herculean haystacks of documents in search of one piece of evidence that may prove useful for a partner's case. Or writing a memorandum on a discrete area of the law that a partner may or may not get around to reading. Not exactly exhilarating work.

If they're lucky, these junior lawyers might have the opportunity to author a minor section of a brief before it gets passed up the corporate chain, never to be seen by them again. In Biglaw, it's not uncommon for a team of, say, twenty lawyers to dedicate years to a single corporate litigation case. Each one of those lawyers will probably toil away at one tiny aspect of the case and never leave their silo, let alone get a chance to take in the larger legal picture. It's hard to feel much passion and commitment when all you do day in and day out is chip away at documents or write an obscure pretrial motion that may have little impact on the case as a whole.

These attorneys often have zero client interaction, which prevents them from learning critical skills or having a connection with the work they're doing. It is hard to feel fulfilled with a legal victory if you've never even met the client or a representative of the client in person.

Malcolm Gladwell once argued that it takes ten thousand hours to become truly great at a craft. In the world of law, that means that, by the end of five years, that team of twenty lawyers might each be good at one very small sliver of the practice of law, but they've been deprived of the opportunity to truly practice law in a meaningful (and well-rounded) sense.

Compare this Biglaw experience to my own experience. While working for a plaintiff's firm in Los Angeles, I had daily contact with the senior partners—just one advantage of working for a smaller firm. The partners ensured that there were opportunities for me to attend trials and to participate in the taking of depositions. In some cases, I was even permitted to argue motions. All throughout, I was interacting and contributing, not just searching for documents.

When I did finally join a Biglaw firm, I was already at a significant advantage. I was well aware that these advantages were not shared by many of my peers; however, even with this leg up, I would have had a difficult path had I remained in Biglaw. The odds of making partner at such a firm were minimal. And often, your skills as a lawyer are just part of the equation on who makes partner.

One reason for that is the organizational systems at most Biglaw firms, where you have the finders, the minders, and the grinders. The finders are the rainmakers: they maintain the big books of business, which provides them with security and the truly big salaries. The minders are best considered service partners: they don't necessarily have their own book of business, but they serve an essential function by managing the cases that the finders bring in. Most associates are grinders. They're the ones in the trenches, doing the work hour after hour, day after day, churning out as many as ten or twelve billable hours a day in order to keep profits streaming in.

As a grinder, it's all too easy to feel like a small cog in a soulless machine. You are far removed from the action, and you might begin to wonder if you even matter. Even partners can feel lonely and lost in the shuffle. A colleague of mine was once employed at a Biglaw firm and was tasked with attending the annual partners' meeting. Hundreds of partners were in attendance, and they all wore name badges. Most had never met one another before.

Nothing about that example says *partnership* to me. My partners and I don't just share responsibility and ownership of Lewis & Llewellyn. We hang out socially, take vacations with each other, and talk on the weekends. We don't just have one another's back; we'd do almost anything for each other within the ethical boundaries. That may sound melodramatic, and, of course, we hope it would never come to that. But the point is that our level of commitment to one another is immense, and we all know and respect each other intimately: the absolute antithesis of having to meet your partner for the first time while wearing a name badge.

And while many of us once viewed attaining partnership at a Biglaw firm as the brass ring, we've also come to realize that the realities are often otherwise. Sure, you can make a lot of money as a partner at a Biglaw firm, but the hours don't get any shorter and the pressure never ceases. And it can be a lonely existence as a junior partner there. You don't necessarily have a reliable book of business, so you don't have job security; you're not considered of a high-enough rank to really be consulted or included by the senior partners. And compounding all of this is the fact that you don't often get to pick your cases. One of the benefits of starting my own firm was that I got to choose the clients and cases where I knew I could really make a difference. Sometimes that means doing defense work; other times it's representing a plaintiff. I can take cases on contingency, fixed monthly fee, or cases that require a hefty deposit. Having the freedom to practice the kind of law I choose, during the hours I choose, and the *way* I choose is immensely empowering. Biglaw simply can't provide those kinds of perks, and I think those perks are a lot more important to being a satisfied lawyer than most people realize.

Undoubtedly, the above factors are why turnover rates at Biglaw firms is so high. Just a generation or so ago, lawyers used to retire from the same firm where they completed their summer internship forty years earlier. Rarely does that happen anymore. Instead, lawyers are encouraged to be as mercenary as their firms, replacing loyalty with a constant search for more lucrative opportunities. And who can blame them? Without anyone working to foster employee satisfaction, without a supervisor or mentor helping you achieve your long-term goals and ensure that you feel fulfilled, why would you feel compelled to stay? Too often, the Biglaw mentality does little more than encourage the idea that all associates are fungible and in service of the greater moneymaking machine.

HIGH BILLABLE HOUR REQUIREMENTS

Once a new lawyer makes it into a Biglaw firm, it may at first seem like the promised land. All the hard work of law school has paid off. And while beginning attorneys are certainly ready and willing to put in the hours, they may not be ready for the minimum billable hour requirements that Biglaw firms employ in order to guarantee a higher profit margin.

The fact is, the entirety of Biglaw is designed around maximizing billable hours. Working late? A dinner will be provided for you as well as transportation home. Need to format a legal brief? The word processing team will take care of that. Computer problem? The tech people will be in your office in five minutes. Everything is designed to maximize your billing, to maximize your profitability to the firm.

I'll discuss the problem of the billable hour in more detail in Chapter Seven of this book. And so, for now, I want instead to focus on the way in which this concept has become the very bread and butter of Biglaw. Typically the minimum is 1,900 to

2,000 billable hours per year, but everyone knows that doing the bare minimum is no way to get ahead. As a result, it's far more common to hit 2,100 or even 2,500 hours in a year. That's not time in the office, time spent on lunches or chatting at the water cooler, but rather, incremental time spent sending an email, taking a client call, or writing a brief. In order to build up that amount of billable hours, junior associates are in the office (or often these days, working from home) a lot. There's a reason that these firms can pay the big salaries that they do.

Of course, this is not to say that Biglaw never provides any opportunity for better experience. Among other things, many firms have great pro bono programs that allow young attorneys to get valuable experience working one-on-one with clients, arguing motions, or even potentially trying a case. At the same time, they get to help the community.

Nevertheless, far more needs to be done to improve the way that young attorneys are treated. Lowering the high billable hour requirements is one obvious avenue for improvement. There are also other important ways to change the culture. For starters, junior associates could be given other meaningful work or at least get more direct contact with the partners. Some law firms now give associates a fully paid vacation, including travel and accommodations, and there have been improvements when it comes to maternity and paternity leave, but there's still more that can be done on that front as well.

In general, the focus on the billable hour encourages inefficiency. Many new lawyers may feel pressured to squeeze out as many hours as they can rather than providing the client with the highest possible value per hour. A culture change (and perhaps a shift in fee structures) could do wonders for employee morale and client satisfaction.

WHY BOUTIQUE?

The word "boutique" gets thrown around a lot these days: there's the stylish, hipster boutique hotels in places like Aspen and Seattle, boutique restaurants offering the latest menus filled with organic ingredients and the promise of careful preparation, and boutique fitness centers offering personalized training and high-end equipment. Hell, I once even saw a dentist office advertise itself as *boutique* on account of its ability to whiten teeth in a spa-like setting.

All that said, I'm proud to call Lewis & Llewellyn a top-notch boutique law firm. Why? Because any client who retains me knows that they can pick up the phone day or night and generally reach me. I'm not going to immediately hand them off to a junior associate while I go after additional clients. Not only that, but each of my clients also knows that they can count on the rest of our firm to serve them as well. They know who is answering the phone and who is handling every aspect of their case. By design, we keep that number of people on any given case to a minimum (often just one or two lawyers) so that those attorneys have the opportunity to become experts on every aspect of our client's case. Because we don't have a bloated payroll filled with junior, mid-level, and senior associates, we can assure our clients a focused legal strategy.

Our clients know that they are getting lawyers well versed in every aspect of litigation and who have built a dossier of experience successfully trying cases. My team is as comfortable in front of a judge as they are in arbitration or drafting motions designed to keep their case *out* of court. We believe in our clients and feel passionately about their cases. At Lewis & Llewellyn, we get to know each and every one of our clients, and we treat them like valued members of our family. We know how much the outcome of their particular cases matters to them, which is why it also matters to us.

Done right, a boutique law firm can truly be the best of all worlds: a commitment to high-quality work, personalized service, and the opportunity for real financial success.

There will always be a need for Biglaw, and that's okay. But we all lose when Biglaw defines the legal world as a whole. Instead, we should all be working to encourage all kinds of opportunities not just for lawyers but also for the clients who need our services. And Biglaw owes it to all of us to do a better job of policing itself and its most destructive practices.

CHAPTER 3

THE LEGAL SYSTEM: HOW WE CAN DO BETTER

"The corporate boardroom mentality and structure encourages companies and the executives to fuck each other...They've invented this new term litigator; what the fuck is a litigator? I'm a trial lawyer. I try cases. There's some lawyers who do nothing but this mediation bullshit. Do you know what the root of mediation is? It's mediocrity. I don't think the trial practice is dead, but it is very ill. There are some days you could throw a hand grenade down the hall at the Harris County courthouse and not hit anybody."

—JOSEPH JAMAIL, JR.

When I need inspiration about improving the legal system, I often turn to the late Joseph Jamail, Jr. Sometimes referred to as the "King of Torts," he tried more than five hundred jury and bench trials, achieving more than $13 billion in judgments for his clients. According to *Forbes* magazine, Jamail himself was worth over $1.5 billion, making him the wealthiest practicing attorney in America and one of the country's richest people.[10] He earned that money being truly great at what he does and never mincing words along the way. Some of Jamail's quotes about the legal profession are quite cutting and observant—not to mention peppered with colorful language. (*Texas Monthly* called him one of "the most artful deployers of the word 'motherfucker'" in the state.[11])

One of my favorite things about Jamail is that he was unapologetically proud of being a litigator. For him, "good lawyer" was synonymous with "good trial lawyer." He bemoaned the fact that trials rarely happen anymore and the fact that young lawyers at big firms today don't have the opportunity to cut their teeth on small cases, which would help develop their skill in the courtroom. I agree.

I'm a huge fan and advocate of the jury trial system; I think it is one of the best ways we have to dispense justice. For one, it's public, and it serves society to have justice that is open and accessible. Secondly, I believe everyone should have the right to a trial by a jury of their peers. In England we don't have that—with very limited exceptions, civil cases are decided by a judge deciding the verdict—and I believe that is a loss to the justice system there.

But while the trial system is fantastic in theory, it is currently broken. It takes too long to dispense justice, it is too expensive (which makes it unaffordable for the majority of people who need it), and it is riddled with frivolous suits. Some of the problems cropping up today aren't merely because of the lawyers involved or the trend toward large corporate firms. The entire legal system bears a lot of responsibility for the situation. But some of the problems *are* brought on by lawyers and large firms because there is no impetus in the legal profession to make the system more efficient, because its current state makes lawyers a lot of money.

Take Jamail's concern that new lawyers aren't being given a chance to cut their teeth on new cases. In movies and television, it seems that every case goes to trial, but in reality only about 1 percent of civil cases make it that far. That means that even lawyers who have been practicing for years lack significant courtroom experience. As a result of this lack of experience, there are few top trial lawyers to go around, which can be a very big problem when a big case comes along. No one wants to put the fate of their company in the hands of an attorney with little courtroom experience. Meanwhile, the few attorneys with demonstrable experience in court are in high demand, and their fees rise accordingly.

This is by no means the core issue with the trial system, but it is a good indicator of how a broken legal system can spawn more problems. At the level of individuals, I do think we have a wonderful judicial system, from talented and committed judges down to skilled and hardworking stenographers. But when it comes to processes and how things play out, most lawyers would agree that inefficiencies, underfunding, and problematic practices have stymied justice and made for unnecessarily long, expensive casework. We make litigation too complicated; we get embroiled in things that don't matter; and we lose sight of the end result: dispensing justice.

So what precisely is wrong with the judicial system, and how can it do better?

THE GROWING EXPENSE (AND TIME) OF TRIALS

One of the reasons that there has been a trend toward fewer and fewer trials is the simple fact that trials have become extremely expensive. Since the system usually functions on a billable hour model, the growing expense of trials also points to numerous delays and long-drawn-out processes; once a suit is filed, it can take years before a trial even begins.

One of the major expenses and causes for delay is discovery. Especially when large corporations are involved, discovery can become an extremely complicated and slow-moving process. Each side is producing documents to give to the other side as well as answering written questions and sitting for depositions.

Document production used to be far more straightforward. You'd go to a warehouse, blow the dust off the lid of a cardboard box, and open it up to find the stack of documents that you needed. In television and movies, the box would always contain the smoking gun that proved your case.

The new reality, however, is heaps and heaps of digital discovery. If you think for a moment about how many emails we send and receive on a daily basis, then you can imagine how many hundreds and thousands of emails there are to sift through in preparation for a trial.

The problem is exacerbated when one side asks for every conceivable document. The result can be overwhelming, a deluge of document production, the vast majority of which have nothing to do with the case. Sometimes, this is undoubtedly a delay tactic on the part of the opposition. But other times, it is most likely either inexperience or incompetence. If more lawyers went to trial, maybe they would have more experience identifying what they really need to win a case. At my firm, we approach a case with the questions, "How are we going to win at trial?" and "What exactly do we need to prove our case?" Being able to hone in on exactly what we're looking for can cut down the amount of discovery considerably.

In 2018, I tried a case concerning a software implementation dispute with over a hundred million dollars at stake. In the end, there were over a million documents produced by both sides. And each and every one of those documents had to be reviewed by a lawyer. Of the million documents produced in that 2018 case, how many were actually used at trial? Thirty. There were thirty exhibits presented to the jury—that's right, during a five-week trial, thirty exhibits. The rest were nothing short of a waste of time.

Although artificial intelligence applications may eventually allow firms to streamline and accelerate the review process, that doesn't solve the problem of wasteful bloated discovery exchange to begin with. Several litigators today are paper pushers; they bury themselves in mountains of paperwork because it is a great delay tactic—and it helps them meet those high billable hours.

This has to change. If lawyers got together at the outset and agreed to narrow their requests for documents, then some of these expensive document searches could be eliminated. It ought to be considered more than a professional courtesy to limit discovery requests and to spare clients and the courts the hassle and expense of these more sweeping discovery dumps.

Of course, even with that kind of agreement in place, discovery disputes will likely still arise. These discovery disputes aren't just the bane of every litigator; they are also prohibitively expensive for our clients. By the time both sides have met and conferred, written letters back and forth, and eventually brought a motion to compel, six months may have passed, all while one side just needed to get answers to a few simple questions or a limited category of documents. While I would love to live in a world where lawyers policed themselves and prevented this kind of scenario from occurring, that's just not the current reality. And so it's up to judges to really hold our feet to the fire and call out lawyers who are knowingly abusing the system.

A recent positive step forward is what is known as an informal discovery conference. Instead of being required to file motions for further discovery, both sides in a discovery dispute can submit a short letter outlining the dispute and then meet with the judge in an effort to resolve the issues. Typically, a judge will hear the arguments from both sides and then state how they would probably rule, were a formal motion brought to the bench. The parties can then either work together to reach an acceptable compromise or pursue a formal motion.

More of this kind of approach to otherwise byzantine legal proceedings would expedite the process and create more affordable pathways for clients.

Another issue that adds to the expense of trials is the length of time it takes to actually get to trial. Even though only about one percent of cases make it to trial, there are numerous delay tactics that lawyers can employ in hopes of wearing down the opposition—for example, filing motion after motion, serving inordinate amounts of discovery, and engaging in unnecessary discovery disputes. Each of these tactics ultimately costs our clients time and money. It's up to judges to do a better job ensuring that cases move along at a decent pace. One solution would be to automatically set a concrete trial date when a case is filed and ensure that that date can only be changed under serious and unforeseen circumstances. Undoubtedly, that would help to focus litigators' attention on what really matters.

FRIVOLOUS SUITS

In addition to the escalating expense of trials, there are also lawsuits that completely lack merit. These cases clog up the system and divert resources from more meritorious cases that need attention, further reinforcing the fewer trials we see and delaying justice.

Lawyers are partly to blame for these issues. Whether it comes from inexperience or because certain lawyers are unscrupulous, there are many frivolous lawsuits brought today in California. If you have $435, you can file a lawsuit. You don't need the facts on your side to file a suit, and far too many attorneys file meritless suits, effectively abusing the system.

In our profession, we are, first and foremost, officers of the court. We should be held to the higher standards that this position implies. Far too often, I see lawsuits being brought that have no credible basis whatsoever. I have certainly been in a situation where I had to tell a client that I was not willing to file a lawsuit because in my opinion it had no merit. And similarly, when I tell clients that the suit brought against them has no merit, they assume that it will be simple to dismiss. But then I have to tell them that it will probably be about a year before we have a credible shot at getting rid of it. And during that year, they are likely to rack up hundreds of thousands of dollars in legal fees even though they did nothing wrong. That is yet another sign that the system is clearly broken.

One way that we could police against this abusive practice is a greater emphasis on the teaching of ethics and civility in the profession (discussed in greater detail below). For several years I was a member of an organization known as the American Inns of Court. Based on the British system of the same name, an American Inn of Court brings together lawyers, judges, legal scholars, and law students to discuss important issues surrounding the legal profession. It's a great way to get to know people outside your practice group and to ensure that everyone understands the importance of playing by the same rules.

As part of the American Inns of Court, lawyers are assigned to a pupillage group: an assemblage of about ten individuals who range from judges and senior lawyers to new associates. About once a month, the group comes together to watch a presentation made by one of the pupillage groups (usually involving comedy) and then to share a meal. Not only does this kind of organization broaden one's understanding of law, but it also builds rapport and reminds us of our shared humanity, regardless of what side of the aisle or bench we may find one another during the workday. I've even had referrals sent by lawyers who are my fierce opponents in the courtroom but were also a trusted peer in my pupillage group.

If we spent more time building relationships with one another, such as the ones fostered by the American Inns of Court, I suspect we'd also spend more time focusing on what really matters—achieving a good outcome for our clients while avoiding the costs, delays and often unnecessary disputes, name-calling, and paper pushing inherent in litigation.

SUPPORTING JUDGES

When we do go to trial, we are putting our clients' livelihoods—and sometimes even their lives—in the hands of judges and juries. Those are roles that come with enormous responsibility. If we want a legal system that works and dispenses justice as efficiently as possible, then it is integral that we treat these roles with the value they deserve.

It's obvious that judges are central to the legal system as we know it, but do we really treat them that way? Most judges are incredibly talented and committed to public service. The pay cut that judges take from comparable positions that they are qualified for at major law firms is substantial. An equity partner in a large firm can easily bring home $2 million or more, while the average salary for a judge in California is about $200,000.[12] That's even less than the starting salary of a first-year associate at a Biglaw firm. Often these judges have decades of experience, and they give up large salaries to devote their lives to public service.

In return, they are often overworked and often bereft of the resources they need. A single judge may be responsible for hundreds of cases at any one time, which makes it virtually impossible for them to give any one of those cases the attention it needs and deserves. It's not uncommon for courthouses to have to reassign cases because of this enormous workload. Conversely, we would all benefit from more judicial oversight and supervision, such as a bimonthly check-in on the case. Unfortunately, the current workload often makes that kind of interaction impossible.

The recent pandemic only intensified this problem. Across the country, backlogs developed in courtrooms handling cases that range from small claims to family cases to criminal cases. Many courthouses were forced to triage cases, which created even longer delays in cases not deemed as high a priority, such as a divorce that doesn't involve minor children or a civil suit.

Even as I write this chapter, most judges still don't have the support that they need, which can make the already lengthy and expensive litigation process drag on even longer. If judges were better equipped to manage the cases brought before them, then the legal system would work much more efficiently. This would improve things not only for lawyers, but for everyone.

It's hard to convince the public to hire more judges. The last thing we need is more litigation, right? Why not build a bridge with that money instead? Obviously, there's only a certain amount of money to go around, but in the end, we are talking about one of the three branches of government here. And it's the one that protects our liberty and our freedoms. It helps us resolve disputes so that we're not out there beating each other with sticks in order to extract justice. Spending more money on judges would allow us to have judges who aren't overworked, so they are more likely to make the right decision and give the cases before them the attention they deserve. That's the outcome that we want and deserve as a society.

THE IMPORTANCE OF JURIES

Jury trials present additional challenges. I'm a huge fan and advocate of the jury system. But my enthusiasm is based more on the concept of a jury trial and less on the current reality. All criminal defendants have the right to a jury of their peers, which is generally interpreted as a representative cross section of the population, especially where ethnicity, gender, and race is concerned. Rarely, if ever, is that the assemblage of individuals a defendant meets in a courtroom. All too often, when friends receive a jury summons in the mail the reaction is twofold: first, complain to me that they have received a jury summons, and second, ask me how to get out of jury service. I myself had the privilege of sitting on a jury several years ago, and it provided a fascinating and highly rewarding experience. I also witnessed first-hand the thoughtfulness, carefulness, and seriousness my fellow jurors put into the process and the deliberations. With the defendant's liberty potentially at stake, the gravitas of the proceedings was not lost on any of us.

By serving on a jury, I also began to understand the ways in which implicit bias can influence a jury. During the case I served, the public defender was drinking expensive, artisan bottled water. For whatever reason, that really annoyed me. I'd like to believe it didn't influence how I perceived her case, but who knows. And it definitely brought home for me all of the apocryphal stories I've heard of lawyers exchanging their expensive Rolexes for $10 drug store watches in an attempt to appeal to a jury, or defense attorney's attempts to make their client look either upright or enfeebled (think, for instance, of the decision to have Harvey Weinstein slowly wheel himself into the courtroom on a wobbly walker, as if that would prove he couldn't possibly be a sex offender). Whether it's dressing a CEO in off-the-rack chinos or insisting that a client wear a wedding band to seem like an upright family guy, so much of a jury trial is nothing short of pageantry and theater. And don't get me wrong: I love it. There is no greater buzz than the excitement of trying a case in front of a jury, nor more anticipation that comes from awaiting their verdict. I wouldn't trade that experience for anything.

During jury selection, however, I witnessed the flimsiest (and sometimes clearly fabricated) excuses from people trying to get out of performing their civic duty. As a society, we ought to see the opportunity to serve on a jury as an honor and a privilege, rather than as a hassle that we need to extricate ourselves from. Instead of viewing jury service as a burden, and waste of time, we as a profession can help to reshape the narrative about the importance of the jury system to society. As lawyers, we have a particular responsibility to stand up and serve when we are called to jury duty.

And employers can also help frame that narrative by emphasizing the importance of jury service and ensuring that employees do not suffer financially should they be called. Offering paid jury service is a values statement about a company. Instead of docking employees' pay or forcing these employees to use personal or sick days, we ought to pay them their full salary and ensure that they are in no way penalized for their time served. After all, companies themselves are beneficiaries of the jury system— cases dealing with contracts, environmental issues, product defects, malpractice, and wrongful termination are brought by or against businesses in civil courts. Wouldn't most businesses want people like their own employees deciding the outcome? Ultimately, we all benefit from having juries that are truly representative of society, not just retirees or a small cross section of employees whose employer happens to pay for jury service.

LEANING ON ALTERNATIVES

It is clear our justice system is currently overworked, underfunded, and victim to a number of systemic abuses that cause the costs of trials to spiral and justice to be delayed. Often the clearest victims of these problems are those who need swift justice, such as domestic abuse victims, but who have little voice to create change.

So while I believe the trial system is the best and most open way to offer justice, there is room for us to lean on alternatives that can relieve crowded dockets and take some of the pressure off the current system.

One of these alternatives is arbitration. Put simply, arbitration is effectively a private trial: it takes place in a conference room instead of a courtroom, but it follows a similar process to a trial. Each side has a lawyer that presents evidence and cross-examines witnesses, and in the end, the arbitrator, who is typically a retired judge, decides a dispute. That decision is both binding and final (which is to say, it cannot be appealed).

Arbitration is fairly common, and whether you know it or not, you're likely subject to numerous arbitration agreements at this very moment. Many credit card agreements include binding arbitration clauses buried somewhere in the nine hundred pages of terms and conditions. The general consensus is that defendants tend to prefer arbitration because they avoid dealing with a potentially impassioned jury that could come back with an extreme verdict. They also prefer it because it takes place behind closed doors.

While arbitration is a great way to help a flagging judicial system, it does have drawbacks that are severe enough to mean it shouldn't be our primary mode of justice. First of all, from a societal standpoint, the fact that arbitration is private means that the public won't know about what happens. Often we will never know about the wrongs committed. Also, it isn't free. Unlike a judge whose salary is paid for by the public, the disputing parties must pay for the arbitrator's services which can easily run into tens of thousands of dollars. Secondly, the ultimate decision is just one person's opinion. While it's true that the arbitrator is a professional, single individuals can reach some, shall we say "unique," conclusions. Something that people don't usually consider about the jury system is that the traditional custom of having twelve jurors didn't arise by chance. That number was determined to be small enough to avoid one or two dominant voices, but it's large enough to avoid the problems of herd mentality. As William Blackstone summarized in his *Commentaries on the Laws of England* from 1768:

> A competent number of sensible and upright jurymen, chosen by lot from among those of the middle rank, will be found the best investigators of truth, and the surest guardians of public justice. For the most powerful individual in the state will be cautious of committing any flagrant invasion of another's right, when he knows that the fact of his oppression must be examined and decided by twelve indifferent men.

Arbitration, by its very nature, does not share that safeguard.

And contrary to popular belief, arbitration does not always provide for the expeditious resolution touted as one of its benefits. While it is true arbitration does usually move more quickly than trials do, especially since there are no appeals, cases can still drag on for a year or two.

Another vehicle to help resolve disputes is mediation. Mediation is essentially a one-day settlement conference. Each party sits in their own room, and the mediator, usually a retired judge, travels between rooms to try to get the parties to reach a resolution. Unlike an arbitrator, a mediator is not a decision-maker; they are simply facilitators. And it is not uncommon for mediations to take place before a lawsuit has even been filed, potentially alleviating further pressure on the judicial system. Jamail may have hated the idea of mediation (as his quote at the beginning of this chapter proves), and in truth his dislike for the current state of mediation is not unfounded. In my experience, mediators are mixed. Some are incredibly diligent. They roll up their sleeves, read every word of the mediation briefs submitted beforehand, and really dig into the details in order to give you an informed opinion. Quality mediators work incredibly hard to get the case settled. But other mediators are just plain lazy. My six-year-old son could do just as effective a job. Poor mediators do nothing but play telephone, passing settlement terms back and forth. I had one very disappointing experience with a mediator in New York, a former judge whose one day's mediation fee was $20,000. Around dinner time, he announced that he was hungry and intended to stop. I politely reminded him we were one block from Times Square and that I was confident we could get some food delivered. On the other hand, I once had a mediator stay until three in the morning because there was a deal to be done. She wasn't going to quit until that agreement was reached. Turning away from the former and rewarding the latter would create better mediation experiences for everyone and would most likely make it a more viable and popular option for lawyers and clients alike.

A third potential tool could be an early evaluation by a judge, almost like an early settlement conference. Every case has what's called, in California, a mandatory settlement conference, but it only happens about thirty days before trial, at a point where both parties have already spent hundreds of thousands, perhaps millions, to get to that stage. But what if we flip it and hold that evaluation early on, when a candid assessment of the case could save a lot of money? Just like setting an automatic trial date when a case is filed, setting an early evaluation could be part of the mandatory case timeline. If a judge takes a look at your case and tells you (or more importantly your client) it's complete bullshit, that could save you months, if not years, of work. And such a conference might ease the burden on the judicial system.

A fourth avenue to easing the burden and increasing the efficiency of the judicial system is the small claims court. This process is quick and cost-effective. In California, for example, the small claims filing fee ranges from $30 to $100, and if you can't afford that you can ask for a fee waiver. You are not allowed to be represented by a lawyer, and once you file papers to start a case, you typically have a court date (trial) in about one to two months, and there is no right to appeal. The downside is that the cap on damages is about $10,000, which means this court is not an option for most plaintiffs. At least in California, this cap has not been revised in years. A simple way to shift the burden of cases from the legal system would be to increase this cap, perhaps to $25,000 or $50,000, diverting cases to this court and making justice more accessible to everyone.

RETHINKING HOW WE OFFER JUSTICE

The unfortunate reality of the United States legal system is that fair and thorough representation is financially out of reach, even for many middle-class Americans. Most individuals do not have access to the civil justice system. Suits for more than $10,000 must be decided within the larger legal system, and it's not uncommon for either side to pay upwards of $100,000 in legal fees, even for something as seemingly simple as a case involving damages after an auto accident. A few lucky potential clients might be able to find an attorney willing to take such a case on a contingency basis, but those lawyers are few and far between, particularly outside run-of-the-mill auto accidents. Meanwhile, corporations are often willing to throw millions of dollars at any suit with the belief that money is no object where legal success is concerned. These two facts have created a legal system defined by profound contrasts and inequities.

Ensuring that individuals have access to justice ought to be the mission of all of us. The same is true for criminal defendants, who are often required to pay for their own expert witnesses and to rely upon either public defenders or a lawyer-of-the-day model, while the state or federal government has access to seemingly unlimited resources. As we used to say in England, in a criminal case you are going up against the entire British monarchy and all of the wealth it maintains. That's hardly a fair fight.

As lawyers, we want to encourage meritorious lawsuits. By streamlining the current system and offering additional paths to justice, including alternative remedies, we can make it a more fair place for everyone. For the judicial system to work, it deserves proper funding and proper attention. That's a hard problem to fix given the current political climate, and when you're an attorney concerned with your own daily grind, but it's something to keep in mind. I certainly don't have a blueprint to fix the entire legal system in one chapter, or even in one book, and it would be arrogant of me to suggest I do. But at the same time, that's not an excuse to not at least identify potential paths forward or to point out ways in which we can work together to keep our eye on the essential goal that keeps society functioning: dispensing justice. We don't have to accept a poorly thought-out system just because "that's the way it is." We can take a cue from Joseph Jamail, Jr. and be more willing to call out the bullshit in the system when we see it.

CHAPTER 4

"THIS IS VOMIT": HOW NOT TO EDUCATE NEW LAWYERS

"Everyone wants to say they hate lawyers, and yet I've never met a parent who didn't want their kid to be a lawyer."

—JESSI KLEIN

In England, a law degree is an undergraduate degree, similar to an American bachelor of arts. It's a largely theoretical degree, which is to say that it's based on the study of basic legal concepts like contracts, property law, and that sort of thing. To become a barrister, an English trial lawyer, a student must then complete an additional year of what we call *bar school*, a one-year training program that teaches more applied skills like advocacy, negotiation, and how to cross-examine a witness.

For me, Thursdays were always the highlight of bar school. That was generally because there weren't any classes on Friday. Instead, on Thursday evenings all aspiring barristers would convene at their Inns of Court. Since their inception in the

Middle Ages, the four Inns of Court—Middle Temple, Inner Temple, Lincoln's Inn, and Gray's Inn—have been devoted to the technical study of English law. In the age before textbooks, law students would be required to eat a certain number of dinners at their Inn of Court, where they would listen to lectures and discussions about the finer points of law. By the time I attended bar school, we were required to attend twelve of these dinners in order to become a better barrister. Did these dinners make us better lawyers? Probably not. But they were absurdly fun.

The evenings begin with a cocktail hour, followed by a formal meal. The bars hosting these barrister dinners always had drink specials, where you could get a bottle of wine for £2, or about $2.50 USD. That is exactly the right price point not only for low-income students, but also for miserly barristers making the minimum rate for practicing cases. After we'd all managed to down our cheap wine, we'd migrate into an imposing hall where the actual dinner would take place.

Everything about these meals was steeped in tradition. At my Inn of Court, Gray's Inn, a wooden screen was given to the Inn by Elizabeth I while she was the Inn's patron, and it is carved out of the wood of a Spanish galleon captured from the Spanish Armada in the late 1500s. Attendees were required to wear robes, and food was passed in a particular way—diagonally across.

But the strangest tradition of all was the prohibition against anyone using the bathroom during what could sometimes be a very long dinner. Of course, you could use the bathroom if you really wanted to, but that meant that the dinner would not count toward the twelve that you needed to become a barrister. The best strategy was to use the toilet at the last possible moment before the dinner started, but you had to be careful because the last person into the room for dinner was called out and labeled Mr. or Ms. Junior. At the end of the evening, all two hundred people begin banging their hands on the table. At that point, Mr. or Ms. Junior would be required to stand up and ask the senior barrister for permission to smoke, which was code for, *May we please use the toilet now?* In response, the most senior barrister, known as Mr. or Ms. Senior, would rise and give a witty speech before granting permission to smoke. As soon as permission is granted, everyone would rush to the bathrooms like a herd of zebras that just spotted a lion.

I want to be very clear here: this was not 1690 or even 1890. Instead, this was the tradition that was alive and well when I attended bar school in the late 1990s. At one particular dinner I attended, a law student at one end of the table asked us all to pass a note down to the senior barrister, who read it, jotted a response, and sent it back. The young man who had penned the original request looked crestfallen. I learned later that he had written, *Please, Mr. Senior, I have a urinary tract infection. May I please have permission to smoke?* The senior barrister's response? *Of course, you may have permission to smoke, but this will not count as one of your dinners.* That's how we train lawyers in England.

Well, that's not all there is to it. But those traditions are reminders that we've taught law the same way for centuries, even as the profession and the world have changed dramatically during that time. Law schools on both sides of the Atlantic are no longer preparing new lawyers for the current realities of the profession. Poor training and lack of preparation may be the reason that so many lawyers leave the profession within a matter of years. There are many ways that law schools can better serve students—and the profession as a whole—by actually aligning to the realities of the modern legal world.

THE ENGLISH MODEL

From the time I was a young boy watching *L.A. Law*, my dream had been to attend law school at Oxford. Our entrance examination included a formal essay written in response to a deliberately loaded question like, *Should England have a monarchy?* Legends abounded about students who had tried to push boundaries with these questions, all in an attempt to get noticed by entrance committees. One of my favorites was the story of an applicant who responded to the question, *What is bravery?* By way of an answer, he simply wrote, "This is bravery" and turned in his essay.

I wasn't nearly so audacious, but I was fortunate enough to be admitted to Oxford University to study law (or as it is known there, Jurisprudence). It was a great time. And absolutely nothing I learned there has any bearing whatsoever on how I practice law today.

I'm exaggerating, of course—but not by much. Most of the Oxford teaching method is based on the traditional tutorial system: as students, we'd be required each week to read a list of articles and cases and then to draft an essay in response. These essays would then be submitted to a tutor, who would then summon us to their office to discuss the draft.

Let me be clear here: when I say tutor, I don't mean some generous upper-class student earning extra money by helping out new students. Tutors in England are typically the reigning authority in their field, and they are very proud of that expertise. Most often, I'd only get out a sentence or two before the grilling would begin: *What do you mean by that? Are you sure about that? What about this case? Why would you think that?* It is a terrifying experience for an eighteen-year-old. But even worse is when the tutor *doesn't* have any questions for you. In one particularly bad meeting, my tutor simply said, "Mr. Llewellyn, this is vomit." I was crushed. But I also learned never to make that mistake again.

I've heard people in the US talk about how terrifying the Socratic method can be in a law school classroom, where a professor might drill down on a case and call on students to defend their views. Maybe. But I'm here to say that those students at least had a decent chance they weren't going to be called on at any given moment. Under the tutorial system, there are no classmates to hide behind: you're getting interrogated, every single week. It's stressful; however, it also builds tough lawyers. As a seasoned barrister once said to me, "There is no greater laxative known to man than your first court appearance." Being cross-examined by the leading authority of any given legal topic at least paves the way for that experience.

After bar school, the next step in becoming a barrister is called a pupillage, which is effectively an apprenticeship. These positions are extremely competitive, and I was fortunate to receive one. A pupillage really just means that you live the life of a barrister for a year. Generally you have a different pupil master or pupil mistress every three or four months for a year, and you go with them to court every day. You observe them, and if you're lucky, you learn to make quite a good cup of tea. I recall once making eleven cups in one day for one barrister. It would be a good skill to have if I liked tea.

After six months in the apprenticeship, i.e., halfway through your pupillage, you are allowed to start trying your own cases. I started out doing criminal prosecution in Essex. Grays in Essex (no connection to Gray's Inn), one of the places where I routinely prosecuted, was recently given the dubious accolade of "the most hideous small town within the British Isles." The typical roster of cases would be a bar fight, someone accused of punching a soccer referee, a bar fight, drug possession, a DUI, and another bar fight. I usually had six or seven trials in one day. I quickly grew accustomed to speaking and thinking on my feet. It was a great experience to be able to try cases at just twenty-three years of age.

My pupillage training was absolutely invaluable in preparing me for a career in law. I worked with four mentors (known then as pupil masters or pupil mistresses) for a year, observing them closely. And halfway through, I was allowed to hone my skills by actually trying cases. In the US, courtroom experience for younger attorneys is the exception rather than the rule. Even as a baby-faced twenty-three-year-old, it didn't take long before my fear of the courtroom went away.

The British legal system is also a very collegial one. Dropping income and increasing workloads have made barristers something of an endangered species in England, so we all tend to know one another and see one another in court. That's very different than here in California, where I routinely litigate against an opposing counsel that I've never met before and will never see again. The smallness of the barrister community breeds collegiality, as does the knowledge that you will undoubtedly appear against colleagues and even friends. Couple that with the fact that a barrister cannot refuse a case that he or she is qualified to take (known as the "cab rank rule"—i.e., taxi rank), and you're bound to find yourself having to leave personal relationships at the door when you walk into a courtroom. Early in my career, my housemate and I found each other squared off in a case (I was serving as prosecutor; he was the defense attorney). During the day, we fought against each other with everything we had. At the end of the workday, we'd go out for a pint like any other set of good friends.

I'm the first to admit that some of the British traditions for educating lawyers are hard to defend, especially if you have a bladder infection. But some are absolutely worth keeping. The more opportunities law students have to practice law, to learn the importance of ethics and civility, and to understand the financial realities of this profession, the better prepared they will be to serve their clients—and their firms.

In today's legal system, particularly at Biglaw, there is so much at stake, and yet there are newly minted partners who have never taken a deposition, let alone tried a case. Right now there's a lot of paper pushing and not as much courtroom advocacy. If people don't have confidence in their ability to try cases in front of a judge or jury, then they aren't likely to be able to give their best effort to their clients. The confidence that I gained through my early courtroom appearances has helped me immensely, and my clients are better off because of it too.

THE US SYSTEM

I did not go to law school in the US, so I can't provide a first-hand opinion on the legal educational system here. That said, as someone who has practiced law in this country for twenty-one years and who has some experience teaching and lecturing at US law schools, I am more than familiar with the product that law schools churn out. I know that some might criticize me and argue that the fact that I didn't attend law school in this country means that I don't know enough about the process to have an informed opinion. However, it's often said that law schools teach students how to think like a lawyer, not how to be one. I don't think you have to attend law school here to evaluate how well it prepares students for a career as an attorney.

As I see it, legal education in the US has some beneficial aspects as well as some aspects that could be improved. The first aspect that needs some kind of fix is the sheer expense of law school. This point is well documented across many different professions. It's not uncommon for people to come out of law school owing hundreds of thousands of dollars. Are we giving those students the best value and the best preparation for that extraordinary cost?

What makes this situation even worse is the fact that law schools aren't even teaching students what they really need. Yes, we teach them the foundations of constitutional law, the basics of contract law and tort, that sort of thing. But the theories of law are only one aspect of this profession.

First and foremost, law students must learn how to *think* like a lawyer. I know this sounds obvious, so let me explain. When I say "think like a lawyer" what I really mean is that law students must learn analytical thinking and good problem-solving skills. They have to be able to view a problem critically, determine what matters most, what solutions are viable, and how to apply those solutions.

Too many would-be attorneys enter law school thinking that we sit around all day, discussing the finer points of a Supreme Court decision and analyzing the opinions issued by the Justices. The reality of my life as a practicing lawyer and the partner of a firm is that I can easily go an entire week or even month without looking at a single case or statute. This is not because I'm sitting in a corner office, sipping Scotch and counting my fortune, but rather because much of my time is spent on the phone, either talking to prospective clients or counseling existing clients on their legal options. Yes, I need to know the law. But what I'm really doing is customer service: my clients have come to me with a problem, and I need to do whatever I can to solve it.

Part of customer service is recognizing that you are in the business of doing business. We may have entered the legal world because of lofty ideals where justice and civic service is concerned, but the reality is that we will only stay in this profession so long as we acknowledge the financial aspect of it. Firms depend upon a constant stream of satisfied clients, but few law schools acknowledge this reality in their curriculum. We ought to be teaching law students how to generate and maintain business, including how best to service clients. What is the right response when a client wants to take an unethical path? How can an attorney salvage a relationship with a disgruntled client? What is the best response to a client who wants to see a detailed budget before a case begins when there are numerous uncertainties in litigation? These are the sorts of issues that attorneys deal with on a daily basis, and yet most of us have received no formal training on how best to handle them.

So many crucial life skills—from effective communication and active listening, to sound investment and time management strategies—simply are not taught in school. That's true regardless a person's chosen profession, of course, but it's particularly notable in the world of law. Many of our clients come to us at one of the most stressful moments in their lives. The majority of them have no background in or familiarity with law, and yet their well-being hangs in the balance there. For that reason alone, it is paramount that we are able to meet our clients where they are, which is to say with knowledge, empathy, and a mutually beneficial plan for going forward.

A law education should reflect these needs. So, too, should the bar exam. Rather than subjecting would-be lawyers to a day of multiple-choice tests, followed by canned essays, why not include practical skills like drafting a motion or a letter to opposing counsel or a client? It's in the best interest of society to ensure that qualified lawyers know how to perform at least some practical aspects of the legal profession before their first day on the job.

THE BENEFITS OF AN APPRENTICESHIP PROGRAM

One aspect of the English system that the American system should copy is the way that new lawyers are paired with more experienced members of their profession in order to observe and learn all the details of practicing law. As a trainee barrister, this is known as the pupillage system. As a trainee solicitor (the other branch of the English legal profession which generally performs work outside of court), this is known as the training contract. During a solicitor's training contract, the trainee will generally perform four six-month "seats" across four different departments of a law firm. For the duration of the training contract, the trainee solicitor will be assigned a supervisor who will set tasks and be available to answer any questions the trainee may have. Having an experienced lawyer to answer questions and offer advice was extremely valuable in my training, and it should be emulated here.

Ideally, this would be a one- or two-year training program in which new lawyers would have the opportunity to try out different practice groups, not unlike the mandatory residencies for new doctors. Certainly there are some individuals who arrive on the first day of law school confident that they want to specialize in tax law or criminal law, but most of us need time to explore the range of options before committing. One of the great hallmarks of a firm that I worked at early in my career was their use of the "unassigned associate." These were new lawyers who had the opportunity to float between different practice groups, such as the litigation, tax, or corporate group, to get a flavor of that area of law and their aptitude for it. That kind of opportunity allows new associates to bank time while developing a broad basis of knowledge: they get to see depositions, attend trials, and sit in on meetings with Fortune 500 clients while making a more informed choice about their own specific career path.

A renewed emphasis on law school professionalism—civility and ethics—during this apprenticeship would also go a long way toward rehabilitating the damaged image of the practicing attorney. There is a trend in a lot of courts, especially in California, to adopt civility guidelines. I find this to be a great idea, but why wait for the courts to act? If the concept of civility is first instilled in law school, then an even greater impact can be made.

A lot of people think that if they have an angry lawyer, they must have a good lawyer. But the complete opposite is true. Lawyers who are adept at civility often have the greatest success. It's possible to advocate aggressively for your client and still maintain a polite and civil demeanor. If we can instill that behavior beginning in law school, it will pay dividends for the profession as a whole. I understand that individuals who go to military academies like West Point here in the US all have to take decorum or manners classes. And you can tell by interacting with them how effective such training can be.

At the firm I joined when I first came to California, one of the founding partners would often grill the junior lawyers and the interns. He'd ask them a question, and their instinct would be to give an explanation. He might ask, "Have you found the answer to this?" and the intern would reply, "Well, I looked here, I looked there." He would stop them and ask again until they actually answered the question with a "no" instead of an explanation about why they didn't have the answer. The training that he was instilling was how to talk to a judge. If a judge asks you a question, answer the question. Judges are professionals, but they can get frustrated. And when they get frustrated or feel disrespected, no one benefits.

During this apprenticeship time, I'd also like to see a greater emphasis placed on career counseling for new law school graduates. Generally, only a small proportion of new associates will eventually make partner, particularly at a Biglaw firm. Since the majority will eventually leave, doing more to retain them or, conversely, to help them consider other career paths—such as going in-house or working for the government—will make everyone happier and more productive. And even if that counseling results in an associate making a radical career change, it's still more likely that that person will refer business back to the firm because their experience there was a positive one.

I know what my skeptics must be thinking right now: this apprenticeship program sounds expensive, especially under the billable hour model. Chapter Seven of this book offers a deep dive on the billable hour, its limitations, and some more productive alternatives. For now, to soothe the naysayers, let me just say that apprentice lawyers would still be allowed to bill, but at a reduced rate more in line with their level of expertise. Lower minimum billable hour requirements would also be key.

Firms could take the training of their newly hired associates more seriously by actively teaching them practical aspects of law. Apprentices could go to court with partners and watch depositions. Such an arrangement could be a fantastic recruiting tool for any firm. In a legal culture that seems all the same to law students, a firm that demonstrated how devoted it was to the development of its employees would set itself apart. It would probably help with retention, since the young associates could build solid relationships with the partners whom they worked closely with.

Could it cost that firm a short-term dip in profits? Certainly, that could happen. But ultimately clients would know that they weren't the ones subsidizing training by paying high fees for undeveloped talent. Ultimately, the profits would hopefully be restored or even surpassed because the firm would be a greater value proposition for clients, and there would likely be a greater rate of associate retention and satisfaction.

In the end, I think we can all agree that having qualified, engaged lawyers skilled at their craft is beneficial to everyone. Part of that skill is knowing not to treat clients like billable commodities, nor employees like cogs in a moneymaking machine. No one benefits from that kind of system: firms face astronomical attrition because of dissatisfied associates; clients feel disempowered and resentful. Obviously, I don't have a magic wand to make these problems go away. But I do know that we need to begin a conversation right now about how we are training new lawyers and the future of this very noble profession.

In an ideal world, law schools themselves would be the driver of this conversation. They all ought to be asking themselves how they can stay current with the realities of the legal profession and its ever-changing identity in the twenty-first century. Centuries-old traditions are great when it comes to ceremonial dinners and even costuming requirements for barristers. But when it comes to preparing new lawyers for a meaningful career, it's time for a new—and far more contemporary—paradigm.

CHAPTER 5

DON'T BE AN A$$HOLE: WHY LAW FIRM CULTURE MATTERS

"Culture either happens by design or default."

—MICHAEL MOGILL

We've all heard examples of notoriously toxic CEOs and the destructive, even demeaning cultures they have created: whether it's the technology innovator who boasts about sexual conquests and misogynistic practices at his multibillion-dollar start-up, the takeout food titan who made not-so-veiled racist comments, or the banking exec who threw lower-level employees under the bus to hide rampant fraud. It doesn't take much for a destructive C-suite to take down an entire company—and the morale of all those who work there. Compare that to the likes of great CEOs like Steve Jobs, Tim Cook, Tony Hsieh, and Bill Gates who encouraged innovation, inspired passionate commitment, and rewarded hard work at every level.

Law firms are no different. When we refer to the culture of a firm, we can mean one of many things. It could be how colleagues treat one another, how we treat our clients, or even how we treat opposing counsel. But no matter what we mean by it, the culture of the firm starts at the top and permeates through the entire organization.

There are some firms that are known for their toxic cultures, and it usually involves a partner who is known to be an asshole. The realities of the legal profession can make it easy for a firm's culture to tip toward toxicity. Big, important cases, tight deadlines, and long hours can create stress and frustration. In firms that don't reinforce a positive culture, the sheer weight of frustration can create tension. A toxic culture can destroy employee morale, wreak havoc on client satisfaction, and spark high turnover rates for both associates and clients.

A positive, productive culture, on the other hand, can make lawyers and supporting staff happier and more willing to go the extra mile. A renewed focus on positive culture will improve lawyer morale, create a place where young attorneys can actually practice law, and promote an atmosphere where people aren't afraid to make mistakes. This kind of culture sets the entire strategic direction of a firm and must come from the top.

So much of the dissatisfaction with the judicial system—both from within and from the public—can be attributed to the culture of the law firm. Unfortunately, a healthy culture is not something that you can create without effort and attention. It's based on daily interactions and decisions and requires constant dedication. You can't reverse engineer a positive milieu; you have to build it one brick at a time.

THE FLAT CULTURE

One of my favorite books is *Extreme Ownership: How U.S. Navy SEALS Lead and Win* by Jocko Willink. A former SEAL team commander himself, Willink led a series of high-stress operations in Iraq. Along the way, he developed real insight into the mind and heart of a successful leader. One of Willink's central tenets is that there are no bad teams, only bad leaders. It's up to leaders to establish clear guidance, to create venues for effectiveness and success, and to encourage positive and productive character traits throughout their team.

In his civilian life, Jocko Willink has become a renowned business coach. Many of his most important lessons come out of his career as a SEAL. He saw firsthand the damage caused when a leader looks to place blame on others for their own foibles, whether it's a commander who blames a failed mission on their battalion or an executive who blames their secretary for a missing memo. A successful business culture, insists Willink, is one in which accountability and responsibility begin at the top.

That same mission ought to be the focus of every partner at every law firm. Far too often, lawyers look for someone else to blame when they mess up. Instead, we need to take responsibility—and that goes double for partners. Even if it's not your case or you never saw the document or particulars in question, it's up to you to take responsibility and ownership for the snafu and ensure its immediate correction.

Like the military, the legal system loves hierarchies. There's no question that leaders are needed, but it's important to remember that reinforcing the hierarchy of a firm at every step isn't necessary and can be somewhat counterproductive. The best law firms are those that exist as flat cultures, where everyone is treated with the same amount of respect and no one is thrown under the bus. Rather than fostering a culture of blame and hierarchical status, we ought to be encouraging one of transparency and accountability.

This includes giving everyone in the team their fair due. For example, I will never in an email or phone call refer to someone as my assistant or my secretary or my associate. Whenever I refer to anyone in an email or in person, I refer to them as my colleague. It goes to the culture that I want to create. We're a flat organization. Everyone in my firm is a valuable member of the team, so I never use titles when I'm referring to my colleagues. When a mistake is made, I am the first to claim responsibility. Not only does that reassure the client, but it sends the message to our firm that we are a team and we look after one another.

I understand that the typical pecking order of law firms—the associate, junior partner, senior partner—doesn't fit with the idea of a flat culture. And now there is a movement at a lot of law firms to call everyone an attorney in order to signal that everyone should be treated as an equal. Such an arrangement does have its drawbacks. If someone is listed as a partner, does that make it easier to get business? Do some clients have the expectation that they will be handled by a senior partner? I'm not sure that's an insurmountable problem. Clients can always be reassured by explaining your experience. But a movement away from formal titles and toward a flat culture will do a lot to make everyone feel valuable and important.

At Lewis & Llewellyn, we go out of our way to encourage this kind of egalitarianism from the start. Whenever we have an opening, we encourage the entire firm to take part in interviewing potential candidates, and everyone knows they have veto power over a potential new hire. Not only does that help our entire team to feel like their opinion is valued, but it also sends a message to candidates that we value them enough to introduce them to our entire team. As we often tell candidates, feel free to reach out directly to anyone at the firm; there are no trolls hiding down the hallway that we are hiding from you.

Does this approach take more time and resources? Sure. Especially if you're conducting six or seven interviews. But the payoff is absolutely worth it in the long run. A job search is not unlike the start of a new romantic relationship: both sides have to think it's a good, compatible fit for it to work. There are no guarantees in the hiring process, but having everyone involved at least makes for a well-rounded interview process and the opportunity to build real consensus around important choices.

From its inception, Lewis & Llewellyn has been built around the idea that ours is a team of equals. In the early days, we couldn't afford full-time support staff, so I was literally going to big box stores to buy supplies, addressing envelopes, and delivering them to the post office or FedEx. In the years since, our staff has expanded considerably, but we still operate under the assumption that no task is below anyone's pay grade—including the partners'.

We also believe that good attorneys aren't born; they're created. Whenever an opportunity arises, I'll ask a junior associate to comment on the draft of a letter, or I'll create opportunities for them to contribute. In the legal world, the culture is so often dictated by the leadership that the other employees feel they have little to contribute or that their ideas are not taken seriously. But bending that curve the other way and asking people for their opinion lets them know how much leadership values their opinion. The added bonus with this kind of culture is that you actually do receive quality second opinions, which only makes you better at your job. Ultimately everyone's work product benefits when you let your colleagues know that you want their honest feedback and that you won't be offended if they tell you something that you might not want to hear.

RESPECTING THE WORKPLACE AND THE WORKERS

I recently saw an article on LinkedIn about workplace dynamics within law firms. The author of the article boiled it all down to one incredibly insightful truism: *there is a direct relationship between spilled coffee on the break room counter and the partnership at that law firm.* The author's point was a crucial one: any partner or executive who thinks cleaning up a spill is beneath them is not someone worth working for. A good leader ought to be willing to do anything they expect their team to do, including keeping the workplace clean and creating a hospitable environment for everyone. If you're the kind of partner who steps over a dirty tissue or walks past a disused cup, assuming that the support staff or custodial team will take care of it, I'm here to tell you that you've got it all wrong. Respect for the workplace and the people who inhabit it must begin at the top.

In a lot of ways, partners are the owners of the firm. And like any other business owner, you have to be willing to jump in and assume any role when need be. That includes helping out someone who is in the weeds or going the extra mile to bring new clients to the firm. It doesn't matter if anyone ever even knows about those efforts: any success is ultimately the firm's success and pays off in the end.

At Lewis & Llewellyn, you can often see me tidying up the office or cleaning out the fridge. I do this not only because it's the right thing to do, but also because I know it will engender a similar commitment in my team. I treat our office like a cherished possession (because it is), and I want everyone else to treat it the same way. It's important that everyone feels a sense of ownership, along with the pride that comes with it. The success of the firm relies upon all of us, so that sense of camaraderie and we're-all-in-it-together is crucial.

I cannot emphasize this enough: how you treat your colleagues, how you treat your workplace, how you treat your clients, how you treat each other, permeates the entire organization. And ultimately it leads to a more fulfilling career, happier lawyers, happier colleagues, greater attention.

So many people, including lawyers who have been practicing for decades, think that being unhappy just goes along with the profession. But that doesn't have to be true. Even with all the stress, lawyers can be happy. If you find yourself working in a firm full of assholes, that's not the profession's fault, that's the firm's fault. That's the culture they have allowed to grow around them. Even if one asshole leaves, there will likely be a replacement asshole along any minute because that's the kind of culture that the firm is willing to accept.

Toxic cultures at law firms are the result of day-to-day decisions, so it's very hard to turn it around without overhauling what decisions are made. It's impossible for an associate attorney to change the culture all on their own. On the other hand, if you are part of the leadership at a law firm, and you recognize that you have aspects of a toxic culture, then it's probably a good idea to honestly assess your own behavior. Even if there aren't any problems, it's always a good idea to ask yourself, *Am I treating my support staff with respect?* Even if your behavior is perfect (which is unlikely), do you tolerate poor behavior from others? Toxic cultures don't usually arise because of conscious effort, but they are allowed to grow through inattention and inaction. Self-reflection is always a good idea, especially if you sincerely want to create the best possible working environment for the people who help you make money.

TREATING PEOPLE LIKE HUMAN BEINGS

It's certainly true that long hours come with the territory when someone chooses a legal career. But there comes a point when leadership needs to understand that their employees are human beings with lives outside of the office. The goal of the profession shouldn't be to burn people out or get them to work as many hours as humanly possible.

As I write this chapter, my partners and I are currently planning a firm retreat in Scottsdale, Arizona. We're not scheduling a packed program in a conference room or a series of lectures on the finer points of law. Instead, we're insisting upon free time, cocktails around the pool, and leisurely meals—all at the firm's expense. Why? Because we believe in the value of building relationships. If our colleagues have the opportunity to spend time getting to know one another on a personal level, they will be that much more committed to working together—especially when shit hits the fan.

Undoubtedly, there will be some week when we're all working on a big trial: no one's had enough sleep, we're running on fumes, and we're all still at the office or hotel conference room when the clock strikes midnight. If we haven't created real buy-in within our firm, it won't take many of those nights before our most valued colleagues begin looking for work elsewhere.

Monthly social events, whether it's a cocktail party or backyard barbeque, help people feel like they are a real part of the firm, and they go a long way toward ingraining that firm's culture. We want every one of our colleagues to be enthusiastic advocates about Lewis & Llewellyn and the work that we do.

Full disclosure: I'm not necessarily a huge advocate of work–life balance. It's a great idea, in theory. It would be nice to work exactly thirty-seven hours each week and to have time to read a book, exercise, spend time with the kids, etc. But there's simply no way to hit those goals week in and week out.

There are simply times when a lawyer and their team has to devote more time to work. For example, when I'm in the midst of a trial, my work is all-consuming. It gets every bit of my attention. I can't simply call it a week after thirty-seven hours and not serve my clients the way that they deserve to be served. At the same time, if one of my children is sick or has a school event, then that's where my focus goes. Trying to balance everything on a daily or weekly basis is just impossible in the legal world and, in my opinion, in life.

But that doesn't mean that work dominates everything. You can achieve a balance in your life as a whole. So you should expect your associates to work long hours when there's important work to do, but you shouldn't require 2,300 billable hours per year because that's going to interfere with their ability to balance their life as a whole. When they are overworked and underappreciated, people work less efficiently and produce lower-quality results. It's important to recognize that there will be times in your colleagues' lives when they simply can't give you their all. And if you try to force them, then you risk burning them out or creating resentment.

When big things are happening in your colleagues' lives, it's important to notice and react appropriately. Are they getting married? What can you do to ensure that they don't have to think about work for even a minute on their honeymoon? If they have a sick family member, what can you take off their plate so that they can focus on what's important to them? When you treat people this way, it helps with retention, and when they are back at full strength, they are happy to give you their absolute best effort. Even doing something as simple as giving them a birthday gift—even a simple gift card—can have a noticeable effect on morale.

Our colleagues are, first and foremost, people. They have a life outside of work and didn't just jettison everything they care about the minute they began working for our firms. We must invest in them if we expect them to invest in us.

Moreover, it's not enough to just invest in employees: to truly foster a humane and supportive culture, we must also invest in people's families as well. A truly functional workplace supports spouses, partners, and family members as well as its employees. Not only is that the right thing to do on its face, it's also the best way to foster buy-in for those difficult cases that require all hands on deck twenty-four seven. Investing in families pays real dividends in the long run. It builds a sense of loyalty and longevity throughout an organization.

When you treat your colleagues as the people that they are instead of sources of profit, then they—and their families—will be happier and more productive. When they know that you understand when they need time off to care for their family, then they won't mind when they have to be in trial for two or three weeks or when you need them to complete an emergency assignment for a client over the weekend. In short, if you help them out, they'll be willing—and even happy—to help you out when the time comes.

If you treat people as merely moneymaking machines, then they can become resentful or even bitter. Such attitudes can work against the kind of culture that you're trying to create. Treating people with respect and recognizing they have an important life outside of your law firm pays dividends in the long run.

CREATING A CULTURE OF OPPORTUNITY

Treating your employees like real people also means providing them with the opportunity to grow and supporting them along that path. A lot of law firms don't take any interest in their junior associates' career development, and that's a missed opportunity. Creating something like a career development program for your employees signals to them that you want and expect them to become better attorneys.

When I was at a Biglaw firm, it was common to receive an annual review that assigned a score from one to five. A partner might come into your office and read you a few sentences. And that was your review. That's not real feedback. It might not even apply to the work that you've done in the past year.

I'm a firm advocate of sitting down with my colleagues and asking them what type of work they *want* to do. I want to know what interests them, and how we can help them with their career. I want to know what they're doing to get their name out there, because if they are doing good work, then that reflects well on all of us.

Many firms don't bother teaching their employees anything but what is necessary to complete a task. But I want to know what my team members want to learn. Do they want to learn how to take a deposition? Are there training courses that they might like to take? This applies to everyone at the firm, including the support staff. Demonstrating that you care about what your people want to learn can set you apart in the legal world.

We also go out of our way to take on any case our associates bring us. Sometimes, these are small matters that wouldn't typically be within the purview of Lewis & Llewellyn since our billing rates might be too high. These cases might not make sense from a monetary perspective, but they absolutely do from an employee satisfaction one. So we're willing to give a discount or expend resources because we want to encourage and reward the fact that our associates have started to generate work.

When it comes to employee feedback, don't wait for an annual review. At Lewis & Llewellyn, we do two formal reviews a year, along with informal check-ins as well. We also have a mentorship program where every associate is assigned a partner who meets with that associate once a month to see how things are going. Those meetings might be as simple as an opportunity to ask, *How is your work going? Do you have too much? Not enough? Are you interested in professional development or speaking engagements?*

It's also important to remember that praise is a powerful motivator as well as a way of letting people know that their good work is getting noticed. At many firms, young lawyers only receive feedback if they've done something wrong. People like having their quality work noticed. It makes them feel appreciated and helps to instill a culture of praise that increases employee satisfaction. When an employee has done a good job drafting a brief or completing another essential task, I also try to make sure to let the client know. Praising your colleagues in front of your clients reinforces their value and lets them know they've done great work.

THE IMPORTANCE OF TRANSPARENCY

A recent article on the legal news site *Law360* sought to diagnose what makes some law firms especially toxic. The authors found several commonalities; chief among them was a lack of openness at the firm. Specifically, they found that a lack of communication, or a bifurcated communication system based on one's rank (communication flows between partners or even partners and senior associates but excludes more junior lawyers) is often to blame. Lawyers interviewed for the article said that this lack of transparency erodes trust and employee morale.

Far too many firms suffer from this problem. Again and again, I hear stories of partnerships who withhold information from their employees, whether it's about compensation, new cases, or even potential company buyouts. That's no way to get buy-in from your associates, your support staff, or their families.

At Lewis & Llewellyn, we've begun holding biweekly presentations where we update the entire firm on the number of new clients, what's going on with current cases, how many clicks our website is getting—literally any information that may be relevant or important to our team. I suspect that some of these meetings include more details than some of my colleagues really care about, but I'd much rather err on the side of full transparency. As a partner in a boutique law firm, a lot of my time is spent behind the scenes, running the firm. I'm thinking about hiring projections, about budgets, about marketing and promotions. I want my colleagues to know about that aspect of the firm, even if it doesn't seem like it will have any immediate relevance in their professional lives.

I also want them to know how determinations are made about salary increases or bonuses. Something about the culture of the legal world makes us all particularly obsessed about money—especially where bonuses are concerned. For that reason, we try to be especially transparent about how any end-of-year bonuses are determined. We'll let our team know the factors we took into account, from how the firm did overall, to the number of hours they billed, to the quality of their performance. We don't just want to announce a number without letting associates know how it was derived.

This kind of transparency must go both ways. By inviting our colleagues to share news and ideas, we also reinforce their importance at the firm. And on more than one occasion, it's been a junior associate or support staff member who has brought a truly winning idea to the table. Just recently, one of our associates proposed a summer equity fellowship to improve access to the legal profession. We thought it was a fantastic idea and are proud to have implemented it.

Culture is the most important thing at a law firm, and it permeates every aspect of the work done there. Every law firm website brags that they have a collegial culture, but simply saying so doesn't make it true. A poor or toxic culture leads to so much unnecessary dissatisfaction. It's time for some serious self-reflection about how we treat one another in the workplace. We must ask ourselves, have we created a culture that is appealing not only to employees, but also to clients? And while nearly every law firm talks about their culture, I suspect few lawyers—and even fewer partners—really know what that concept means, let alone how to foster a positive environment.

As much as we might like to, we simply cannot sit down and design and implement a positive culture from the get-go. Instead, it is built with each priority set and every decision that is made. Beginning with how we treat one another within the firm, we can make simple changes that pay big dividends.

Far too many lawyers are willing to put up with a toxic workplace because they feel like they have no other choice. That's bullshit. No one should be willing to put up with abusive or even dysfunctional behavior. If you are a lawyer at a firm with more than a few assholes, ask yourself if you are truly willing to tolerate that. There are plenty of great firms out there doing truly quality work and populated by happy lawyers.

On the flip side, if you're a partner in a firm, you owe it to your entire team to ask yourself to what degree you might be creating a destructive culture: Do you shout or demean your colleagues? Are you treating your support staff with consistent and appropriate respect?

Regardless of your seniority, taking some time for self-reflection is key here. Ask yourself to what degree you are responsible for your firm's culture and to what degree you can effect change. If the answer is *not much*, it's probably time to look elsewhere. If the answer is more than that, it's time to take positive action to create the kind of place where people truly want to work.

The COVID-19 pandemic has made this kind of reflection all the more important. So many people became accustomed to working from home, and the pandemic revealed some real imbalances about expectations for time spent either at the office or even just commuting to get there. As a result, we're all now experiencing a tension between people wanting to get back to the office and people who want to continue working at home. More than a few companies are resorting to carrot-and-stick approaches, trying to find promotions or even bonuses for people willing to be in the office three days a week.

That's the wrong approach.

Company leaders, whether they are C-suite executives, partners in a law firm, or even the owners of mom-and-pop stores, ought to be doing everything we can to create the kind of collegial, rewarding culture that has employees eager to be at work. Our colleagues ought to want to come into the office, interacting with one another and feeling rewarded for their time. If being dressed from the waist up and sitting in a bedroom on a Zoom call sounds like a better alternative, we've failed them. Collaboration, teamwork, and innovation are the lifeblood of any organization. Try as we might, that just can't be replicated on a video call.

CHAPTER 6

―――

"IT WOULD BE MY PLEASURE": HOW WE OUGHT TO BE TREATING CLIENTS

"We put clients first!"

—EVERY LAW FIRM WEBSITE EVER

Whenever I embark upon a new case, I often begin by looking up the opposing legal counsel: I want to get a sense of who they are, their background, and their experience. Just recently I visited the website of a new opponent and found this language: *Our core philosophy is to approach the practice of law from the client's point of view. This unique client-centered method allows the firm to manage each case in a way that is carefully tailored to serve the particular needs and objectives of each individual client.* Stop the presses! A law firm is making decisions based on the needs of their clients? That's incredible—and most certainly worthy of some kind of award.

I'm being facetious here, of course. But whenever I see some kind of language about a client-centered approach, I always think, *Thanks, Captain Obvious*. I mean, what else would they put first? Their golf game? It's such an obvious concept. Do these firms actually think they've somehow unlocked the secret weapon to being a great lawyer? Has our profession become so driven by ego that we think considering the needs of our clients is actually a novel or innovative approach to the practice of law?

I sincerely hope not.

The fact of the matter is that we all should be putting our clients first. The practice of law is ultimately about customer service, and most firms would do well to take a lesson from our corporate cousins on this front.

Take the wildly successful story of Zappos. As their longtime CEO, the late Tony Hsieh, told the *Harvard Business Review*, the company reached a real crisis in the years after its founding.[13] Even with generous return policies and easy online ordering, many Zappos customers wanted to talk to a real human being, and the online shoe seller wasn't set up to handle a robust call center. Executives considered outsourcing calls to India or the Philippines, where wages are significantly lower, but decided that that wasn't the right move. Staffing a call center in the Bay Area was prohibitively expensive, both for employees facing exorbitant cost-of-living rates and a company competing with hugely successful start-ups. So they made the audacious decision to move their entire company to a location where focusing on customer service representatives could take precedent— Las Vegas. As Hsieh explained, "We settled on Las Vegas for a number of reasons. It's an all-night city where employees are used to working at any hour, which would help us find people willing to take the overnight shift. And because so much of the city's economy is focused on hospitality, the city has a customer service mentality—employees there are used to thinking of people as guests."

Not only that, but Zappos changed their website to make sure that their telephone number and email are prominently displayed at the top of every page, and they committed to staffing their calling center twenty-four hours a day.

But that was just the start. Zappos got rid of canned scripts and expectations for call times. They encouraged their representatives to take all the time a customer needed and to respond to their needs. In that *Harvard Business Review* article, Hsieh listed just a few of the many examples of customer service provided by these representatives: hours spent helping a woman select a pair of heels, flowers sent to a customer who had lost a beloved family member, and even recommendations on where to find late-night restaurants. Yes, that kind of service goes above and beyond. And that is precisely why every law firm should be paying attention to it.

Whether you realize it or not, law firms must now compete with the Amazons, Southwest Airlines, and Zappos of the world. When it comes to customer service, clients compare us not to other law firms, but rather, companies such as these. It's not enough to be slightly more responsive than Jones, Smith & Jones; instead, we have to provide the same attention and care these clients receive every time they walk into an Apple store. Only by adopting such a mentality and culture will a law firm truly thrive.

What makes that even more of a challenge is the fact that clients often turn to us in states of extreme stress. If a family member has just been arrested or died, if your spouse has run off with your neighbor or your business partner has fled with the company earnings, you most likely already have some pretty significant trust issues. That means your attorney is going to need to go the extra mile to make you feel heard.

CLIENT SATISFACTION IN THE LEGAL INDUSTRY

One tool successful companies use to gauge customer satisfaction is the Net Promoter Score (or NPS). A measure that's used to gauge customer satisfaction with a company, NPS scores are calculated by asking customers one simple but very important question: *on a scale from 0 to 10, how likely are you to recommend this product or company to a friend or colleague?* The results are then sorted into three categories: promoters (9–10), neutrals (7–8), and detractors (0–6).

Promoters aren't just loyalists, they're evangelists (or as we say later in the book, members of your cult), the kinds of clients who bring you new business. Passives are satisfied with your services, but generally unenthusiastic. Detractors, well, detract. They probably won't come back, and they might drive away other business.

To calculate your law firm's NPS, subtract the percentage of detractors from the percentage of promoters. This will give you an NPS score ranging between negative 100 to positive 100. For example, if 43 percent of your clients answered 9 or 10, and 18 percent answered 6 or below, then the NPS for your law firm is 43 minus 18, which is 25.

According to Law Technology Today, the legal industry currently has an NPS of 25, putting it in line with airlines, wireless carriers, and credit card companies. Meanwhile, companies known for excellent customer service and incredible business growth, such as Amazon, have NPS scores in the 60s or higher.[14]

The good news for law firms is that the bar is significantly lower, and if you take some of the steps that I suggest, it could make a substantial difference in how your customers view your firm. Why is this important? The NPS focus on promoters is key. Highly satisfied customers become important promoters of your business. When someone needs an attorney, your firm's name will be on their lips. That positive word of mouth is good for business. A concerted focus on client satisfaction sets you apart from other firms, who, most likely, aren't putting in the effort necessary.

And the statistics back up just how important customer service can be to consumers. According to studies, 50 percent of people would pay for a better customer experience. People are also four times more likely to defect to a competitor if a problem that they experience is service-related. And 89 percent of clients stopped doing business with a company because of poor customer service.

These numbers aren't specific to law firms, but there's no denying that customer service can make or break any business. The realities associated with law firm client satisfaction are no less stark. Consider this: the average number of people that a satisfied client will tell about your firm is nine. The average number of people that a *dissatisfied* client will tell about your firm? Sixteen. That's almost twice as many.

CUSTOMER SERVICE AT THE MANDARIN ORIENTAL HOTEL

I want to start with an example of extraordinary customer service from outside the legal industry because it exemplifies exactly the kind of customer experience that we should all be aiming for. The story comes from my favorite book on customer service, *Never Lose a Customer Again* by Joey Coleman.

Coleman tells about a time that he stayed at the Mandarin Oriental Hotel. Since he hadn't been feeling well before his flight to Las Vegas, he grabbed some cough syrup, took a swig, and then tossed the bottle into his bag of toiletries. He arrived just before he was scheduled to speak and quickly dropped off his luggage in his room. But when he opened his toiletry bag, he discovered that everything was coated in a sticky, pink goo. The cap of the cough syrup had come undone, and the result was a major disaster—one that he didn't have the time to deal with. He set the bag on the bathroom sink and went off to give his talk.

When he returned to his room later that evening, he found that the housekeeping staff had done a turndown service. Resting on a towel on the bathroom counter were all of his items, entirely free of the pink goo that he had been dreading dealing with. Even the offending bottle of cough syrup had been restored to its former state, complete with the tiny dosage cap. Coleman was astonished that someone had tackled the huge mess. But then he found the note. It read, "I hope you are feeling better, Mr. Coleman. Signed, Kelly."

As Coleman points out, the Mandarin Oriental Hotel didn't train its staff on how to clean a bag of toiletries that had been soiled by a rogue bottle of cough syrup. It would be impossible for anyone to anticipate the millions of things that could possibly go wrong when someone comes to stay at your hotel. But they did train their staff to be observant and to be proactive when it comes to customer satisfaction. Kelly's decision to go above and beyond what is normally expected of a hotel housekeeping crew created such a memorable and fulfilling experience for Joey Coleman that he used it in a book on customer service.

The opportunity to create such memorable experiences doesn't come around every day, so you have to pay attention. A few weeks ago, I was on a Zoom call with a client, and I noticed a chalkboard behind him that said, "14 days till Cabo!" I picked up on that and asked him about the trip, including where he was staying. Fourteen days later he arrived at that hotel and found a gift card for the resort spa and a note wishing him a wonderful vacation.

Anyone can create memorable, positive experiences for their clients. It takes a little effort, but it's well worth it. You just have to be observant. On a Monday morning, take the time to talk with your clients about what they did that weekend. Engage in conversation not only to be friendly, but also to find out more about them. If you can create a remarkable customer experience, something unexpected, then you know they're going to remember it for a long time—and tell others. Why shouldn't we hold ourselves to that bar that five-star hotels hold themselves to?

I've given presentations on how to bring the hotel service experience into the realm of law firms. As I tell my audiences, we all ought to be striving for the Ritz-Carlton experience. At the Ritz-Carlton, all the team members, from housekeeping to bell boys, are empowered to do whatever it takes to help a customer. They don't have to go through layers of management in order to get approval. If a guest requests something, they aren't allowed to say yes or no; they always respond with, "It would be my pleasure." That's the kind of culture that law firms can build in order to set themselves apart.

To achieve that level of customer service, law firms must begin at the top: partners need to educate themselves about best practices in customer service before training their employees. The best approach is to take a page from corporate models, which begin with goal setting and the creation of action plans, followed by training, implementation, and thorough assessment, all in the name of continuous quality improvement.

THE CLIENT'S EXPERIENCE

Tailoring corporate customer service expectations to the legal world is easier than it sounds. The first step is recognizing that most clients undergo a seven-step process that begins with discovering that they need an attorney and concludes with the resolution of their legal matter. I call this *the client's journey.*

Each of these seven steps is an opportunity for a law firm to provide world-class service while enhancing the client's satisfaction with the firm.

RESEARCHING FIRMS

In this day and age, the overwhelming majority of clients search for legal representation with a simple Google search. What that means is that your first point of contact with any potential client will most likely be your website. Even knowing that, many firms invest precious little money and resources into a quality, responsive website. Instead, they rely upon a few stock photos and some generalities about the legal services they offer, their success rates trying cases, and the fee structure they offer. No wonder many consumers compare us to used car salesmen—it looks like we're using the same playbook!

The website of a customer service–minded firm should make that mission clear from the start. Your site should not only convey specifically what your firm does, but also your emphasis on client satisfaction. Have you provided a clear client service statement? Does your homepage explicitly state that client service is a priority? A quality website will also include client testimonials and photos of your team interacting with those clients.

And while it may sound obvious, it's also important to take a cue from Zappos and ensure that your phone number and email address are easily accessible. I'm always surprised and disappointed to see how many law firms don't include that information front and center. If a prospective client can't reach you, how could they possibly hire you?

INITIAL CONTACT

Communication is vital to creating a positive client experience. Research has found that about half of all law firms take three days to respond to a query from a potential client, and many of those responses are from a remote case screener, not a lawyer.

Even when someone refers a client to you, it's useful to ask how and when that initial contact is being made. How quickly are you responding? Again and again, I respond to an email from a potential client, and I get a note back that says, "Thank you so much. You are the first lawyer who has gotten back to me." That always astounds me. When I see a subject line that says "potential referral" or "potential case" I drop everything to respond. My response will be the first human touch that person has with my firm. If it takes me two or three days to get back to a potential client, I'm giving them the impression that they just don't matter. Whenever I hear someone say, *I can't believe I'm talking to a partner*, I know my extra effort has been worth it.

Think of how you like to be treated as a customer. For instance, I hate being put on hold. Just the other day, I was on hold with a major credit card company. The stated wait time was ten minutes, but it ended up taking over an hour. By the time I finally reached a customer service representative, I was beyond frustrated and felt like my time had been wasted. It doesn't take many of those kinds of frustrating experiences to add up to a negative reputation.

I'm not suggesting that just because someone reaches out you have to take their case, but a quick reply explaining why you won't be able to take them on as a client is also a simple courtesy that leaves a good impression. Whenever possible, I always offer a referral if we aren't able to take the case: the next time that individual needs an attorney, we want them to consider us.

THE FIRST MEETING

Meeting with an attorney for the first time can be a nerve-racking experience. Law firms can make that experience even worse by scheduling a meeting based on a lawyer's convenience, rather than the client's. Too often, those meetings are either conducted by junior associates or screeners; just as annoyingly, they can also be rushed and driven by a lawyer's arrogant assumptions, rather than what the client wants or needs. The client leaves feeling frustrated, and the lawyer missed an opportunity both to build rapport and get a better understanding of the case.

Compare that experience to one of a service-minded organization. At that law firm, meetings are scheduled at the clients' convenience. The firm is ready for that appointment five minutes early, and a partner joins the lawyer who will serve as the key point of contact in welcoming the client. They work together to understand the client's ideal outcome, and they practice active listening to ensure they understand the client's needs. They also take the time to explain the legal process, fees, and any other pertinent information.

One question that I find useful to ask when I initially meet with clients is, "What's your ideal outcome here? What are you looking to achieve?" Too many lawyers assume that they know what's best, but a client's expectations can help inform your strategy. For example, they may want to avoid litigation at all costs, or they may want to fight to the bitter end. Getting as much information about what a client wants can help to manage their expectations. It's also important to be clear about what they can expect. Many clients are shocked at how long litigation can take and will quickly redefine their priorities once faced with that information. Far better to have that opportunity at the start, rather than once a case is well underway. Similarly, understanding the limits of a client's budget is important very early on. Good communication means clearly conveying the costs for each potential scenario. It's easier to build a successful long-term relationship if a client has realistic expectations about the costs involved.

This may sound obvious, but dress like a lawyer, even if this first meeting is on Zoom. It's what the clients expect, and it shows that you are ready to meet their expectations. Imagine that you were getting on a plane and the pilot entered the cockpit wearing jeans and a T-shirt. That choice isn't going to inspire confidence.

At the end of your first meeting, make sure clients have the opportunity to ask all the questions they might have. And it's always a good idea to reassure them that they can call or email if they suddenly think of something that you didn't cover.

It's also worthwhile to ask your new clients if there's a particular way they like to be contacted. Do they prefer a phone call? Do they like email, or even text messages? Ask them how often they want to be contacted about their case. Do they want every last detail, or are they fine with being updated only on the big picture issues?

FINALIZING THE ENGAGEMENT

It always shocks me to hear about how few firms follow up with a prospective client after their first meeting. It's as if some lawyers have decided that their expertise and mere presence on this earth are so valuable that clients will be clamoring for the opportunity to engage their services.

I'd love it if that were true someday. In the meantime, we all need to be hustling to secure a new relationship. In addition to following up after an initial meeting, we should also be making it as easy as possible for clients to execute an engagement letter. I like to use Docusign so that they can have the option to sign electronically instead of having to hunt down a scanner to complete the process.

When a client has formally retained my services, I like to send a handwritten note of thank you. It's just a memorable gesture that conveys how much we appreciate them putting their trust in our firm. In addition to expressing my gratitude, this note is also an opportunity to reinforce that I am always available to address questions or concerns.

WHEN WORK IS ONGOING

If you haven't attended law school, legal proceedings can seem like nothing short of a dark art. Most clients are unclear about the shape their case will take, necessary steps along the way, and the timeline involved.

It's our job to keep them informed along the way. If you set a time frame, be sure that you are able to meet that deadline. If you say you can have something for a client in a week, then be sure to do so. Emergencies happen, but you don't want to be known as someone who overpromises and then delivers two days late every time.

Since litigation is such a long, drawn-out process, it's also helpful to check in with clients to ensure that they still have the same goals as they did when the case started. It's fairly easy—and completely fair—for a client's goals to change during the course of litigation, but it's the attorney's responsibility to make sure that the goals of both parties are aligned.

As a case moves forward, I reach out to clients and ensure that they know what's happening, when it's happening, and why it's happening. The advantage of detailed communication is that, when the bill comes, there's nothing new. You've already discussed what has transpired and why it was necessary. Ideally, clients will look at the bill and find exactly what they were expecting. If clients ever ask me what's happening with their case, that suggests that I haven't done my job in keeping them updated. I want to be out in front with the things that they want to know.

Billing descriptions provide an opportunity to communicate with clients about their case. Detailed explanations can provide a lot of information and prevent miscommunication. I've seen billing descriptions from some firms that say simply "work on case." What does that mean? How can a client evaluate that? I review every word of every bill before it goes out in order to make sure everything is clear. I also ensure that the bill is sent out promptly. Some firms take three months to send a bill. There's no reason to delay, especially since clients will call with a question, and you have to think back three months instead of having the explanation fresh in your mind.

No one likes to give discounts, but occasionally and for the right client, it's a good idea to surprise them. Everyone expects a Christmas card in December, but no one expects a 10 percent reduction on their legal bill in March. Those unexpected discounts cost the bottom line a bit, but they also keep you top of mind as far as your clients are concerned. You can simply omit charges for some services with the same idea. It's never a bad idea to let an important customer know that you appreciate them.

CONCLUDING THE ENGAGEMENT

At the end of an engagement a lot of firms drop the mic and head out, and clients never hear from them again. What those firms may not realize is that they've forfeited valuable opportunities not only to continue their relationship with that client, but also for that client to refer the firm to others.

At Lewis & Llewellyn, we always take the opportunity to debrief with a client at the end of an engagement, and whenever possible, we try to do so in person, either at our office or, if it's appropriate, over lunch at a nice restaurant. This meeting is yet another opportunity to remind them that you appreciate their business; it's also an opportunity to ask for referrals or to explain other services offered by your firm.

If your client has been victorious, consider sending a congratulatory letter or gift. If they were not, be sure to get feedback from your client about their experience. Sometimes, based on that feedback, we'll make adjustments to their final bill, particularly if the client is less than satisfied with the representation they received. I'll also be sure to include a personal note with that last bill.

POST-ENGAGEMENT

Don't be afraid to ask your clients if you can subscribe them to your newsletter. Even if they never open a single email, your firm's name will stay in their mind. And there's nothing wrong with sending former clients a quick note if something relevant comes up. I personally maintain a spreadsheet with pertinent information about my clients and their families. I may drop a note on a wedding anniversary or send a small gift on a baby's first birthday.

I also try to keep Google alerts that are relevant to the case—

and our mutual opponents. Depending upon the nature of your relationship, this can be helpful information or even the opportunity to take a lighthearted jab. Recently I noticed that a major company that we had sued was celebrating the opening of a new location with a lot of celebrities in attendance. I sent a quick note, quipping about this so-called hottest ticket in town to my client. It was an opportunity to share a quick joke about our mutual adversary. It also reminded that former client that he was still on my radar, which couldn't hurt.

Too many of us take client service for granted. It's not just a slogan that you paste on a website; it's a commitment to service culture that requires everyone at a firm to contribute. We can't rest on our laurels and instead must actively work to create a positive client experience. It's an investment well made: not only does it pay key dividends, but we all benefit in the end. Studies have found that loyal, satisfied clients are four times more likely to refer business to their law firm. Those numbers speak for themselves.

For a true service culture to thrive, the entire firm needs to buy in. You can't just have one or two people who are good at customer service. For it to really have an impact, you need every point of contact in your firm to be on the same page, to be ready and willing to provide the Mandarin Oriental experience. Always create opportunities for your employees to provide feedback and new ideas—and don't forget to listen to these ideas and look for ways to implement them. Take the time to explain your service expectations and how they can be met by the entire firm.

Lead with positivity, and always be on the lookout for those unexpected opportunities to provide value. You want clients to be surprised by the things that you do for them. Your goal should be to leave a client as surprised and satisfied as Joey Coleman was when he found an eight-word note from Kelly at the Mandarin Oriental Hotel.

CHAPTER 7

BILLABLE WHAT? HOW BEST TO ACCOUNT FOR YOUR FIRM'S TIME

"If you want an adventure, join the Navy. If you want short days, leave the law. It's a demanding profession and will become more so in the next century. Every year brings stories of lawyers abusing the chargeable hour…If your compensation is tied to hours, you may round up rather than round down. It is as if you were allowed to grade yourself in law school. It's a disturbing problem that many lawyers don't want to acknowledge."

—LATERAL LINK, "LAW FIRM HOURS – THE
REAL STORY," *ABOVE THE LAW*

There's a story that I heard Tony Robbins tell years ago about a huge overnight shipping company that had a mechanical problem at their sorting facility. This company flew in packages from all around the country, unloaded them and then loaded them onto their destination planes—all in one night. But when their entire conveyor system suddenly stopped, it looked like they were in for a disaster. If the packages couldn't get out they stood to lose millions.

The owner of the company went to his mechanical team, but they couldn't figure out how to get things running. Finally someone suggested the owner call one particular mechanic who knew the system well. Out of desperation, the owner called the guy in.

The mechanic showed up, looked things over, and then pulled out a screwdriver. He reached deep into the mechanical workings and tightened a single screw. And just like magic, the conveyor belts jumped back to life.

The owner was ecstatic. "Great work," he told the mechanic. "What do we owe you?"

The mechanic put away his screwdriver and said, "Ten thousand dollars."

"Ten thousand dollars," the owner exclaimed. "You've been here three minutes and you turned one screw!"

"Sorry," the mechanic said. "But it's ten thousand dollars."

The owner couldn't believe it, but then he thought that he could outsmart a mechanic any day, so he asked, "Can I get an itemized bill for that?"

"No problem," the mechanic said, and he found a napkin and jotted down his itemized bill, handing it to the owner. When he was done the owner looked down at the bill and sighed. He walked away, only to return in a few minutes with ten thousand dollars in cash from his office safe. The mechanic thanked him and left, a giant smile on his face.

A stunned vice president of the company went up to the owner. "I can't believe you paid him that. What did the bill say?"

The owner handed over the napkin, and the VP read it:

Labor: $1

Knowing which screw to turn: $9,999

This apocryphal story illustrates an important point to remember when it comes to billing. You don't only bill for your time. You also charge people for your knowledge. And sometimes that knowledge is extremely valuable. In the case of the shipping company, the knowledge that it took to fix their conveyor system was worth far more than the amount the owner eventually paid.

For some clients, a lawsuit may be the largest financial investment of their lives. It can mean the difference between survival and closure for a business. It could mean the difference between a loved one living free or spending a lifetime in prison. As lawyers, we have become complacent in believing that the billable hour is always the right approach. Along the way, we missed the benefits—both to clients and our firms—of finding better billing models.

THE BILLABLE HOUR

I realize that I'm not the first person to write about the drawbacks of the billable hour in the legal profession. In fact, dozens—if not hundreds—of articles have been written on this subject. I certainly don't want to imply that I've had some unique insight into the problems associated with this type of fee arrangement. It's been written about many times before.

At the same time, the billable hour is still the dominant system in the legal world. With that said, I do have experience with offering clients a menu of fee arrangements. I've listened to client feedback on this issue, so I think that I have something to add to the well-worn discussion of the billable hour as we know it.

It's valuable to recall that the billable hour hasn't always been the method that lawyers have used to bill their clients. Lawyers once considered the value that they delivered and then presented clients with a single bill. The switch to timekeeping as the industry's primary method of billing took hold by the 1950s. It still manages to hold on despite the fact that it's fairly unpopular among both lawyers and clients.

Under the billable hour model, lawyers must account for our time, typically in six-minute increments or one-tenth of an hour. What that means is that, at the end of each day, we have to break down each and every task we performed and assign a time increment to it. It is an exceptionally tedious and time-consuming process: the task of billing alone, especially if you work on multiple matters in a single day, can easily take fifteen or twenty minutes per day or more. Keeping track of the billable hour also acts to commoditize our knowledge and the service we provide.

But there are more general problems as well. For one, hourly billing makes it so that lawyers and clients have two different goals in mind. The firm wants more hours, so the profits are greater. Meanwhile, the client wants fewer hours to keep costs down. Secondly, hourly billing focuses on efforts and activities, as opposed to the most important thing for the clients: results. This misalignment of the goals of lawyer and client can lead to friction in the relationship, a prime cause of dissatisfaction. Finally, the billable hour doesn't measure the actual value that a lawyer provides for a client.

Here's an example of what I mean by the billable hour not providing a measure of value. I was in Las Vegas a few months ago when I got a call from a client who was working on business transaction that was worth tens of millions of dollars. He explained that the other side was getting cold feet and signaling that they were going to back out. "Paul," he said, "we need you to write a letter that firmly explains to them what will happen if they don't go through with the deal." The client had called on a Saturday afternoon and caught me sitting poolside at my Vegas hotel. But he was also a very good client, so I said, "No problem." I wrote the letter in about an hour and sent it to the client. "Looks good," he said. "Send it out." The next week I spoke to him and asked if the letter had worked or if I needed to follow up on it. He told me that the letter had done the trick. The merger had gone through.

That letter helped save a multimillion-dollar deal; however, I could only charge one billable hour—the tiniest fraction of what it was truly worth for my client. Compare that to an hour I might spend responding to emails or shuffling exhibits in a deposition. It's not that I'm not working in this latter example, but what kind of value and expertise am I really providing to my clients for that hour? There's a great deal of variance in how much value a specific amount of an attorney's time provides for a client, but the billable hour assumes that every hour is worth the same amount.

Billing by the hour can place more risk on the client's end since there's always the possibility that a particular matter will take much longer than anticipated. The only person who has to pay for that overage is the client, even if they didn't necessarily receive more value for their money. The arrangement fosters a production mentality as opposed to an entrepreneurial spirit.

Another criticism of the billable hour is that it penalizes efficiency. If one lawyer can finish their work quicker than another, then the result is that they are actually paid less for their output. There's no incentive for lawyers to spend much energy learning to work more efficiently. Is there a better way to approach billing that can work to align the goals of lawyers and their clients?

As the focus on billable hours has increased, firm profits and associate salaries have been rising. Typically, large firms require that associates bill between 1,900 and 2,000 hours each year, and those numbers are up from just a decade ago. The starting salary for a brand-new lawyer from the class of 2021 at Biglaw is generally $215,000 per year. That's for someone who has been practicing law for all of twelve weeks. The rising salaries for inexperienced lawyers do not reflect the value that those lawyers can provide. There's so much money to be made that firms are happy to match the bonuses that other firms give their associates, which only serves to inflate the salaries more.

It's important to note that the Biglaw firms don't hand out these large salaries because they are kind and benevolent entities. They can do it because the billable hour requirements have gone up. And even though salaries are up across the industry, that doesn't mean that the status quo is the optimal situation for each individual. Imagine an extremely efficient superstar associate who is adored by clients and produces consistently superior output. They deliver value, get along with their colleagues, and help the team as much as possible. At a Biglaw firm, that superstar attorney would be penalized because he or she would be making the same as an average attorney who didn't provide nearly the same amount of value.

From the firm's perspective, the billable hour can place an artificial ceiling on total income. There are only so many hours in the day to be billed—or so it seems. I've heard more than one story about attorneys logging six minutes of time for each one-minute email they send. Do enough of those, and it can look like you're working more hours than there are in the day. One of my favorite examples is that of a lawyer who was hard at work while on a transpacific flight. At some point, the plane he was on crossed the international dateline, which meant the lawyer charged his client for twenty-six hours worked that day.

I realize that Biglaw firms are doing pretty damn well right now because of these systems, but it's certainly a point that they should consider. A more common problem for firms is that the constraint of the billable hour penalizes advances in the firm's effectiveness. In other words, the faster a firm can solve a problem either through better trained or more knowledgeable employees, the less the firm earns. Inefficiency is rewarded, so there's little incentive to improve. That arrangement isn't good for clients and is probably one of the reasons that clients dislike the billable hour system so much. When was the last time you paid for a haircut, a lawn mowed, or even a meal at a nice restaurant based on how long you received service? That may work for spas and ski slopes, but it's no way to run a railroad.

CONTINGENCY AND FIXED FEES

When working on contingency, a lawyer takes on the risk, and in exchange they get a percentage of the recovery, typically one-third. Working cases on the contingency has the great advantage of aligning the lawyer and client toward the same goal. The more money the client gets, the more money the lawyer gets. Efficiency is also rewarded. Ideally both the clients and attorney want to get the case to victory as quickly as possible. In addition, contingency fees reward lawyers who are willing to take on risk.

Unfortunately, contingency fees only apply to plaintiffs. What if you find yourself as a defendant? There's no payment at the end of the case, so there's nothing to split. In cases like this a fixed fee might be a better option. A lot of lawyers say that they're scared to death of fixed fees. "What if the amount of work goes over the fixed fee that I quoted my client?" they ask. Well, it can be risky, but it's good to remember that fixed fees are the standard across all kinds of industries. If airports or skyscrapers get built for a five billion–dollar fixed fee, then it should be possible for lawyers to litigate using the same arrangement.

Conversely, sometimes clients approach me and say, "Okay, Paul. What if you send one letter and the other side immediately settles? Doesn't that mean that you just made a huge amount of money for almost zero work?" I have two simple responses to that question. First, if only I were that good! I'd be sitting on a beach in Hawaii, writing the occasional letter that causes my opposition to immediately fold. Second, I tell them that they are equating my time with my experience. A letter may take me only an hour to write, but it's the twenty-three years of legal experience that makes the letter effective, not the hour spent writing it. What you are buying is knowing what to put in the letter. Just like the mechanic in the opening story, the knowledge provides the value. When you retain my services, you are buying the gravitas of my law firm. You're paying for my first-rate education and the wealth of experience I've gained.

If you need open-heart surgery, you're not going to find the cardiologists with the lowest rates; instead, if you're like most people, you're going to find the one who's the most qualified to complete the procedure. That surgeon knows how to save your life because she has probably done thousands of similar surgeries before meeting you. You can't place a price on that kind of value.

Of course, some lawyers worry fixed fees will work against them—and the amount of work they have to put into a case. I'll admit that's possible, but in my experience it's also very rare. Nuclear power plants, bridges, high-rise skyscrapers, and satellites all get built on fixed fees. Do we really think we can't litigate a legal case using the same system? Rarely are cases as uncertain as these kinds of infrastructure projects. And like the contractors who complete that work, we can build in guards against high levels of uncertainty, such as starting with an hourly basis to get the lay of the land or reassessing a contract annually or even quarterly. You can also set fixed fees for different stages of the case.

It's also possible to work out a monthly fee schedule based on your estimate of the average monthly cost for similar cases.

Structuring fees this way helps to guard against a case that drags on far longer than you were expecting. Fees could also be task-based, so that depositions, motions, etc. all have a set price.

At my firm, we find that clients like the certainty that fixed fees provide. It's much easier for them to budget for their legal expenses. They do tend to ask about what happens when a task takes much less time to complete. Aren't we just making money for doing nothing?

My response is that being on a fixed fee schedule makes me feel unshackled. I want to litigate without thinking about what my decisions might do to the bill. Being free from the constraint of the billable hour allows me to deliver as much value as a particular case needs. And that's not just what I tell clients, it's how I actually feel. When I do sit down and compare the fixed fee to what the cost would have been had I billed clients hourly, I find that I actually do make a bit less. But the freedom is worth it for me. I'm free to do things in litigation that I know clients would probably not want to be billed for. I don't want to ever feel uncomfortable about doing the best thing for my clients.

Fixed fees are becoming more common, and more clients expect them. There are a lot of benefits that might not seem obvious at first. At Lewis & Llewellyn, what we tend to hear from clients is that they really appreciate the certainty of the fixed fee system. It's so much easier for most clients to budget for legal fees when there aren't any surprises. As a lawyer, I'm less worried about bills with a fixed fee, and I can dedicate far more of my time to being the best litigator I can be. I don't worry about whether or not a client wants to pay for a certain service or communication and, instead, I just stick to doing whatever best serves that client and their case.

Another fee arrangement that we've used, primarily on the defense side, is the early resolution success fee. If the firm gets rid of a case early on—say within the first three months—then the firm gets a bonus. This helps to realign the interests of attorney and client, since clients want cases to go away as quickly as possible, but attorneys make more money the longer a case drags on.

Of course, some opponents of this model argue that lawyers shouldn't want to get rid of a case quickly, for example by cutting corners, particularly if they are representing a defendant. To that I would counter that a good lawyer is always giving everything they can to their clients and would never dream of cutting corners or compromising the well-being of anyone they represent. Obviously I'm going to do the best to resolve the case for my clients no matter what, but if a case does take a long time it might be natural for clients to wonder if we're really doing our best.

In my experience, clients appreciate fixed fees and other fee arrangements that move away from the billable hour. As the rate for billable hours rises, clients are beginning to question the value that they receive under such a system. It won't be long before even Biglaw firms will be forced to rethink their billing strategy as the demand for change grows.

Along the way, there are simple steps we can all take to normalize these options. From a strictly semantic standpoint, I'd love to see the legal world do away with verbiage like "alternative fee arrangements." The very use of the word "alternative" suggests that the billable hour is the norm. I'd like to argue that we reverse that expectation and use billable hours as the exception to the rule.

The billable hour probably still has a place in the legal world, but we are best served by giving clients more options. I'm certainly not an advocate for the death of the billable hour, but I'm also not an advocate for the belief that it is the only—or even the best—way forward. Lawyers tend to be risk averse and unwilling to change when it comes to questions of billing. There are multiple alternatives to the billable hour, and we need to embrace and adopt them where they make sense. We need to move closer to the true value that we provide to clients apart from the time we spend. After all, the turn of a single screw can be worth thousands. But we don't always have to charge that much.

CHAPTER 8

"MY LEARNED FRIEND": CIVILITY IN THE COURTROOM (AND BOARDROOM)

"Civility stands for nothing more complicated than lawyers treating each other and the system of justice with professional courtesy and respect."

—LEE COOPER

It's been years since I have practiced law in England; however, my barrister wig still maintains a position of prominence in my office. It's not because it's particularly comfortable (in fact, the horsehair is miserably scratchy—not to mention oppressively hot during the summertime). The wigs are also inconvenient to cart around and expensive to purchase or replace—about $1,500 for a basic one. Nevertheless, when anyone surveys the British people, both barristers and their clients resist the idea of doing away with these accouterments. Why? Because the wig and barrister gowns both add an important element of gravitas to legal proceedings. They remind us all of the solemnity of the occasion and the importance of decorum in every interaction.

I'd argue that the English system reinforces civility far more effectively than the American system does. In the UK, lawyers are required to bow before judges whenever they enter the courtroom. In addition, the rules of the court require that you refer to your opposing barrister as "my learned friend." The terminology alone diffuses a lot of tension. The word "learned" shows that you respect their intelligence, while the word "friend" creates an atmosphere of polite respect.

No, I don't think we should adopt the phrase "my learned friend" in the American system. But those English customs can remind us that the courtroom doesn't need to be a place of hostility or nastiness. Too many lawyers operate under the misconception that being aggressive will benefit our clients. In fact, the opposite is true: we can use aggressive tactics, but we will almost always get better results if we are collegial with our opponents.

On more than one occasion, I've had potential clients tell me they're looking for a real pit bull or ballbuster: a lawyer who is willing to be aggressive and to take no prisoners in the name of a client's case. I've also seen attorneys who believe that yelling or lobbing ad hominem attacks is the best way to demonstrate they're committed to winning their clients' cases. In both cases, people are wrongly confusing aggressive tactics with outright aggression.

Don't get me wrong: no one wants a mild-mannered litigator, and a milquetoast approach in the courtroom won't get you anywhere. In litigation, there can be only one winner, and no one wants to be on the other side. Of course, you want your client to win. And a good lawyer will advocate fiercely for their client. That's appropriate.

What is never appropriate is being an asshole.

THE RISE OF INCIVILITY

It's fair to say that few, if any, lawyers or judges would say that lack of civility isn't a concern of the legal profession today. For decades, bar associations, judges, courts, and commentators have all lamented the decrease in civility across the field.

What do we mean by civility? Justice Anthony Kennedy described it as "respect for the individual, respect for the dignity and worth of a fellow human being." And I'd like to add my own erudite definition of civility: "Don't be an asshole." Unfortunately, I have witnessed firsthand the lack of civility in the legal profession on an almost daily basis.

Why is diminishing civility an issue? John Silber, the seventh president of Boston University, put it this way: "The lawyer's contribution to the civilizing of humanity is evidenced in the capacity of lawyers to argue furiously in the courtroom then sit down as friends over a drink or dinner. This habit is often interpreted by the layman as a mark of their ultimate corruption. In my opinion, it is their greatest moral achievement. It is a characteristic of humane tolerance that is most desperately needed at the present time. Yet something has gone amiss." That quote really speaks to me based on my experiences in the English legal system. I know how great a civil system can be for working lawyers, and it's a shame to see things headed in the opposite direction.

There are opposing views, however. As one attorney explained in an article in the September 1999 issue of the *National Law Journal*, "I am a trial lawyer. If you are my opponent, I don't care if you like me or find me witty, or engaging. We're not going out to dinner. We're not friends. All you really need to know about me is this: I will beat you if there's any way the rules will let me. I get annoyed and sometimes genuinely infuriated at the self-anointed 'civility police' who lately have pitched their tents at our local bar associations."

It probably goes without saying that I think that this guy has it all wrong. His embrace of a "win-at-all-costs" mentality and a needlessly aggressive attitude toward his opponents is never acceptable. It's fairly simple to not be a jerk, but he is embracing the role of jerk because he cares more about his ego than he does about the profession. He ignores the fact that he is an officer of the court.

What happened? How do we get to this stage? First, this kind of attitude is reflective of the national culture as a whole. The political system is broken. People in general have little respect for their elected officials or for institutions. Everything is black and white, where blind loyalty to political party, or the prospect of reelection, relegates national interest to a very distant second place. There's a reason some people only watch Fox News and others only watch MSNBC. They want to consume media that reinforces their own viewpoints, and there's little interest in understanding why others think the way that they do.

The prevalence of anonymity online has also fed into the rise of incivility: people can comment on photographs, leave restaurant reviews, or share their opinions all behind an avatar and without fear of being discovered. I've seen anonymous comments left about me that describe me as greedy or disgusting. Never once did those cowards have the courage or dignity to pick up a phone or send an email saying as much.

Within the legal world, there has also been a real failure to mentor at law schools in this country. Even though the rise of incivility has been noted for years, I'm not aware of any requirement in law school that students receive any guidance on the issue. And the transition away from law as a profession to law as a vast moneymaking operation is partly to blame. Instead of elevating the concept that lawyers are, first and foremost, officers of the court, the mentality of winning at all costs has become the dominant force in many areas of the legal world.

LACK OF CIVILITY HAS A COST

It may seem like the rise of incivility is no big deal, but it does have real costs to lawyers, clients, and the profession as a whole. Being a jerk costs money because it leads to unnecessary disputes that waste the time of clients and the courts. How many pointless email arguments have been charged to clients over the years? These heated disagreements can lead to bringing unnecessary motions before the court or engaging in delay tactics, or even using up deposition time simply to insult your opponent. Does being a jerk ever actually help your client?

Being the angry guy in court can also be bad for your health. A Harvard Medical School study showed that the risk of having a heart attack is significantly higher following an outburst of anger.[15] Hostility and lack of civility can literally be a life-or-death issue.

I've already talked about how stressful the legal profession can be. The lack of civility only makes that problem worse. In fact, the rise of incivility makes a lot of problems in the legal profession worse. Clients are hit with rising costs, and trials get delayed by petty disputes that could be easily resolved if both sides were willing to work together.

Some of the jerkier lawyers probably don't realize that their attitude costs them money. About 95 percent of my referrals come from attorneys at other firms. If everyone thinks you're a jerk, no one is going to send any business your way. Lawyers with a poor reputation for civility are shooting themselves in the foot. And that's apart from them creating a poor work environment for everyone else.

I've witnessed my fair share of hostile, boorish behavior from my fellow attorneys. I've had lawyers shout at me on the phone. I've had lawyers insult my intelligence. I've had lawyers threaten to sanction me for daring to bring a lawsuit. I've had lawyers accuse me of not knowing the law because I was educated overseas. Some lawyers will go to the greatest depths if they think it might give them an edge.

The proliferation of email as a means of communication has made civility problems worse. It's very easy to send out an angry, inconsiderate email without thinking about how it will be received. It sometimes happens that I'm pleasantly surprised by someone's in-person demeanor after dealing with them over email.

I recently read an article about an attorney who was producing some documents for the other side in a case. When they realized that the attorney worked just across the street, they decided to drop off the documents in person. From that moment on, the tone of the case changed, becoming much more friendly. And that was based on just a few minutes of personal conversation. Not much, but enough to remind both sides that there were real human beings involved in the case.

It's a good idea to remind yourself of the humanity of your fellow lawyers. We can all get frustrated in this stressful job, but remembering that each of us is a human with a family can help keep everyone grounded and reinforce the kind of civility that we all want to see.

It's true that sometimes clients can get the wrong idea if you have a good working relationship with opposing counsel. I've been in depositions that have gotten quite heated. And then when there's a break, the other lawyer and I are joking around with one another. My clients often say to me, "How can you do that? How can you just turn it on and off?" And I explain to them that you can advocate strongly for a position, but it doesn't mean that the other person is a bad person. I actually enjoy going out to dinner with opposing counsel after a case is finished. Some clients do get suspicious, but when I explain that aggressive advocacy does not mean aggressive personality, it tends to reassure them. Shouting at your opponent actually hurts your case.

HOW WE CAN IMPROVE

In a 2021 California Court of Appeal decision, the court wrote, "We publish this decision as a cautionary tale. The timbre of our time has become unfortunately aggressive and disrespectful. Language addressed to opposing counsel and courts has lurched off the path of discourse and into the ditch of abuse. This isn't who we are." And isn't that true? This isn't who we are. We can do better as lawyers. We can do better than treating each other as punching bags and thinking it's legitimate to demean, disrespect, or be rude to our opponents. We can do much better.

How can we do better as a profession? I've touched upon one of the areas already, and that's law school. We can begin rehabilitating the profession by making civility part of the legal curriculum. We want to ingrain these concepts into the next generation of lawyers, that being an effective lawyer does not mean being an aggressive person. It does not mean acting rudely to your opponent. It would also be worthwhile to include civility training as part of the continuing legal education that practicing lawyers are already required to complete. Is two or three hours every couple of years too much to ask?

A lot of state bar associations have adopted civility guidelines, and while I agree that this is a laudable goal, in my opinion, a lot of those guidelines only pay lip service to the problem. How many lawyers really sit down every few months to refresh their memory on the finer points of the San Francisco Superior Court's civility guidelines? It's fine as far as it goes, but I don't see it as a viable solution.

A more realistic response would be for judges to begin enforcing civility more often. If judges started sanctioning lawyers who breach decorum, or at least if they call such conduct out, then maybe the culture could begin to undergo some real change. These monetary sanctions could help to steer behavior back toward civility. Bar associations often discipline attorneys, but they are very unlikely to punish someone for incivility alone.

Can we do better as a profession? Yes, but it's going to take every single one of us. It starts with how we treat the profession, how we treat each other, and how we mentor and train younger lawyers. We need to be willing to call out incivility when we see it, whether from our opponents or from our own colleagues. As the former United States Solicitor General John W. Davis said:

> We build no bridges. We raise no towers. We construct no engines. We paint no pictures. There is little of all that we do which the eye of a man can see, but we smooth out difficulties. We lead stress, we correct mistakes. We take up other men's burdens. And by our efforts, we make possible the peaceful life of men in a peaceful state. Isn't that the real calling of our profession?

As lawyers, we help society to function. Isn't that one of the most noble callings that any man or woman can do? Can we resume our role in society? I believe we can. We don't have to accept the current lack of civility as permanent. We can, and we should, focus our efforts on smoothing out the difficulties—not only the difficulties of society, but the difficulties among ourselves.

CONCLUSION

The judicial system is sick. Too many lawyers are dissatisfied with what they're doing and how they're doing it. From training lawyers to serving and even billing clients, there are ways to improve ourselves and our results. We can treat each other more humanely and commit to customer service. We can foster an environment in which everyone—from partners to recruits to support staff—feels empowered and encouraged to work and grow.

It starts with us, the members of this great profession. We must learn to be proud of our history and our important place in society. Bad-mouthing the profession only hurts us in the long run. It's incumbent on each and every one of us to do better.

I'm just one kid from England who really liked an American TV show, and now I'm practicing law in California. I recognize that I don't have all the answers to the problems that plague the legal field, but I do have a unique and varied experience. In each of the preceding chapters, I attempted to tackle a broad aspect of the field, but I know that there is much more that could be said.

So many lawyers are dissatisfied with what they're doing, and it's easy to see why. The dominance of Biglaw and the emphasis on profit and hours has made many lawyers feel like tiny cogs in a giant machine. The lack of funding in the judicial system itself adds stress to the job. Hours are long, and the demand for more hours can make the job seem more like a grind than the passionate vocation that it should be. And on top of all that, some of our fellow lawyers feel the need to heap abuse on us in order to gain advantage.

At the same time, there is much room for hope. Despite the public's perception, our profession is filled with amazing and dedicated people who provide enormous value to the clients they serve. If these talented people come together to help reform the way we educate lawyers, future generations won't have to suffer the indignities that occur in today's environment. Partners at law firms can help immediately by taking proactive steps to rebuild their firm's culture around positivity and collective success. We can do more to rehabilitate the public perception of lawyers by treating our clients with more care and offering better customer service (yes, lawyers do provide a service, and it behooves us to hold ourselves up to certain standards). And we can all strive to be kinder, even as we prioritize the needs of our clients and advocate fiercely on their behalf.

Of course, some of the issues with the justice system are beyond our control. No individual lawyer has the power to hire more judges or allocate more public resources to the system. That takes widespread political change. But we can advocate for alternative methods of justice to reduce the burden on the trial system and focus on discovery that speaks to the heart of the case, instead of just being paper pushers. We can create the impetus for change, even if it is not endemic in the system.

And change *is* possible—Lewis & Llewellyn is proof of this. My dream was always to have my own law firm. And when I finally set out to do so, there was no guarantee of success. I decided from the beginning that Lewis & Llewellyn would practice law at the highest level and compete with any firm in the country. But I wasn't going to sacrifice my principles to make it happen.

I haven't had to. I'm proud that my firm has been able to build a culture of respect and support—I would literally trust my law partners with my life. The fact that everyone on the team has each other's backs helps to ease the stress inherent in the big cases that we take on and helps us make a difference one client at a time. This is especially true for the type of cases we handle including our niche practice group representing survivors of sexual abuse. I'm enormously proud of what we've been able to accomplish. Approaching each client with empathy and understanding and listening closely to their concerns—and doing it at every level in our firm—allows us to be the best attorneys that we can be both in and out of the courtroom.

Just recently, the *National Law Journal* named Lewis & Llewellyn one of America's elite boutique law firms. We were thrilled to see our personalized, high-end service and top-notch legal work recognized. But as great an honor as that accolade was, what really motivates me is hearing praise from satisfied clients or other members of my firm. Part of the reason that I wrote this book is that I want every lawyer in America to have the same feeling of support, mutual respect, and impact that I enjoy.

Because let's face it: to excel at this job, you need commitment. As someone who has, through fortune and hard work, been able to make a successful career in law, I know the amount of dedication it takes. No matter how much you think you know when you step out of law school, it's not enough. You have to work like crazy and never stop learning. There is no instant gratification and no shortcuts. If you plan to dabble at law in search of a hefty paycheck, you won't get very far. You have to have a passion for doing the absolute best for your clients, for going above and beyond—only then do you have a chance at a successful career.

Given that level of commitment, shouldn't we all want to find real joy in the work that we do?

The good news is we can, but it begins by stepping away from the status quo. Don't listen to those who tell you, "But this is how it has always been done." So what? How it has always been done is often archaic, damaging, and sometimes a bit silly (remember the "may I have permission to smoke" story?). It certainly isn't the best way. You don't have to accept toxic situations—there are better ways. Fight for them.

This fight is worth it, and it is not just because ours is a truly noble vocation, one that requires a lifetime of dedication. It is because, on a simple individual level, fulfillment in your career translates into your life. How many of us dread Monday mornings, celebrate the weekends, and work on autopilot for a paycheck? If you consider that an average workday is eight hours long—and that number is a lot higher if you are a lawyer—how many hours of our lives is us being "switched off," plodding along, and accepting mediocrity?

If you fight for excellence, however, for work that fulfills you and gives you genuine joy because the field respects and supports you, then these hours invigorate you. They give you more energy to spend on your partner, your kids, your friends. They make your life better.

It also teaches you to go after what you truly want, not what you've been told to want. Throughout this book, we've talked about the issues in the legal profession and industry, but if I had to boil my message down to a single sentence, it would be this: don't settle for this crap. You don't have to agree to or accept this system because "this is how it is." You don't have to march along the set path because it was outlined for you in law school. Or because your parents thought it best. Or because society says this is what "success" looks like. Ask yourself what you truly want—what ignites you?—and then *chase* it. Not just in your career, but in every aspect of your life. Build the life you want to live, one that is true to you. There is no other way to live with passion and dedication—and that is a life you deserve.

BONUS CHAPTER

RED, WHITE, OR NEITHER: THE POWER OF THE GIFT

When I wrote this book, my focus was on how lawyers could create a fairer and better legal system that serves the interests of all stakeholders: the public, lawyers, firms, judges, and society as a whole. But what sometimes gets lost in these conversations is the business of law: the act of providing a service to people and keeping that service going. So I want to leave you with something to think about as an individual who is part of or runs a business—because, believe it or not, that is exactly what we do as lawyers.

Let's talk about gifts.

We've all been there: every December, a deluge of e-cards inundates your inbox, each one wishing you a very happy holiday from one firm or another. It's quite possibly the most generic holiday greeting you could receive, made all the more so because you know that, somewhere on the other end, a support staff member or attorney simply chose an online card template, downloaded an email contact list, and then pressed send while the partners congratulated themselves for a job well done wrapping up end-of-year communications with their most valued clients.

Many of the actual gifts sent out by firms are no better. In my time as a lawyer, I've received countless bottles of forgettable wine and boxes of mediocre chocolate by the truckload (as if any of us needs more calories around the holidays). I've received notifications that donations have been made in my name to goat sanctuaries (nothing against goats, but I've definitely never asked for that) and meat and cheese baskets that look like they've been beamed here from 1963. All of these overtures may have been well-meaning, but they absolutely fail at what ought to be their primary purpose.

As far as I'm concerned, we give gifts in the professional world for two main reasons: to thank or acknowledge someone with whom you've done work, or to generate future business. We send professional gifts to express appreciation and keep our firms or companies in the minds of people who might need our services later. Sending a generic e-card or a room-temperature sausage and some processed cheese isn't going to do either.

One of my favorite voices on the subject of gift giving is John Ruhlin, author of the bestselling book *Giftology*. In it, he outlines what makes a good—and bad—gift. Take that bottle of wine, a perennial favorite gift given by companies. As Ruhlin explains in his book, it's a flawed gift for multiple reasons. First, a sizeable amount of the population doesn't drink. If they do drink, they reach for beer or spirits and not a cabernet. Even if they like wine, you don't know if they prefer red or white, sweet or dry, full-bodied or smooth. The likelihood of multiple recipients thinking you've just sent them the best bottle of wine in their life is infinitesimal. The other reason something like wine is a terrible gift is because it is incredibly forgettable. By its very nature, a bottle of wine (or box of chocolates or basket of processed cheese) is meant to be consumed. And once it is, the recipient will most likely never give it a second thought.

If you're trying to achieve either goal of gift giving—expressing thanks or driving business to your firm—you need to start thinking differently about giving. Too many of us exist on autopilot mode, just doing what all the other firms do and have done since the beginning of time. That's the wrong approach. At Lewis & Llewellyn, we do not give holiday gifts. It's not that we're Scrooges, but rather, because we don't want to get caught in the same rat race as every other company. There's such a flood of gifts at the end of the year that any one is bound to get lost. Knowing that, we tend to send out gifts twice a year and at off-peak times, like March and October. Why? Because no one else sends gifts in those periods. Straight away, that puts us ahead of the crowd and helps our gifts get noticed. And because those are not traditional gift-giving times, our offerings have the extra benefit of surprise. The recipients feel like they are getting something out of the blue, and that adds to the element of thoughtfulness.

We also put a lot of time, effort, and thought into these gifts to ensure that they are something people will actually want and will use again. As John Ruhlin contends, one of the best gifts you can give is a kitchen knife. Why? Because it's something we all use again and again. And the best part of that gift is that it's not just used by the direct recipient, but also by that person's spouse and children. You've reached not only that individual, but also that person's inner circle, and that helps show you really care.

A few years ago, we decided to try Ruhlin's idea: we sent out high-end kitchen knives as a thank-you gift to our clients. In return, we received all kinds of photographs of people using their knives (or at least *pretending* to use them). We also got emails from clients that said things like, *my partner says that every time he/she uses this knife, they think of your law firm.*

That is why you spend so much thought trying to settle upon the perfect gift.

Gifts should be useful—and something that the recipient will use often. They should reflect the time and energy you put into them. Everything about receiving a gift—from the quality of the wrapping paper to the gift itself—should be a pleasurable experience. At Lewis & Llewellyn, we don't think twice about agonizing over the thickness of tissue paper or the color of the cardstock we use to write a handwritten note. That's not because we're obsessive (well, only with respect to our cases); it's because we understand how much the thoughtfulness of a gift experience really matters.

If there's one type of gift I believe in above all others, it's the gift of extraordinary thoughtfulness, or the "GET." Let me give you an example. A potential client tells you he's an avid runner. You could send him a coffee mug printed with your logo, but that would have zero resonance in his life (and who needs another coffee mug?). You could also send him a subscription to a running magazine. That subscription doesn't cost much more than the coffee mug, but it's an infinitely better gift. Not only will the potential client think of you each month when a new issue of the magazine arrives in their mailbox, but they'll also do so with the recognition that you have gone above and beyond: instead of something generic, you've actually taken the time to think about who they are and what they want.

This isn't hard to do. If I know a client is going on vacation at a specific hotel, I might arrange for a voucher at the hotel spa to be waiting for them when they arrive. While Zooming with a lawyer who has referred a lot of cases to me, I happened to notice she was wearing a Harry Potter T-shirt. My colleagues and I went online and found a signed copy of the first book autographed by Daniel Radcliffe, who plays Harry in the films. We ordered Hogwarts wrapping paper to ensure the lawyer would have the full Harry Potter experience. All said, we spent about $1,000 on the gift, but the amount of meaning we gave to that lawyer was priceless. That ought to be the key element of a gift: it has great meaning for the recipient.

Of course, giving a gift of extraordinary thoughtfulness requires you to know something about the recipient. This also isn't as difficult as it may seem. The first few minutes of many phone or Zoom calls is spent making chit-chat: often, the person on the other end will talk about how they spent their weekend or what their upcoming travel plans might be. Social media profiles often include a person's hobbies or interests. Other opportunities abound to find out if a person has a family or what they like to do on their weekends. This isn't magic. Instead, it's about taking the time to pay attention—and to remember what you learn. Using a spreadsheet to keep track of a person's significant other or when they've had a baby can go a long way toward showing you care not just about their business but also about the people who most matter to them. For instance, whenever we learn that a client has just had a baby, we'll send an infant-sized robe with the baby's name on it. Then we record the date of the baby's birth and follow up a year later with a birthday card.

Involving a person's inner circle goes a long way toward making that person an advocate for your firm. More than an advocate even, you want that person to become a devotee—or, as Michael Mogill, founder of Crisp, puts it, you want that recipient to want to become a member of your cult.

I know what you're probably thinking: there are absolutely no reasons why you'd want your firm associated with a cult, which immediately brings to mind a group of religious fanatics brainwashing impressionable people to join them. That's an unfortunate association, says Mogill. He points out that our culture is actually brimming with cults: Nike, he points out, is a cult. Apple is a cult: why else would people camp out on a sidewalk overnight just for the opportunity to buy their newest phone the day it's released? Thought of that way, a cult is simply people who believe in your product and are willing—eager, even—to advocate for that product.

That kind of endorsement ought to be the goal of every law firm. We want our clients, and even our prospective clients, to be fans. We want them to advocate for us and, in the end, to choose us when they need legal services. We want them to recommend us to others and create an exponential impact by telling everyone they know how wonderful we are so that those people become our clients too.

This doesn't have to be with actual gifts or cards either. As one marketing expert recently put it, the number one piece of mail people open begins with, *you're invited*. People love events. Don't get me wrong: I've certainly been to more boring networking events than I can count: you stand around and make awkward conversation, trying to balance a glass of that mediocre wine (leftovers from the holiday gift giving, maybe?) and a plate that's a bit too small to actually hold hors d'oeuvres. You don't want to eat anything, for fear that someone will approach you while you have a mouth full of food. You leave not having made a single meaningful connection, and yet the event was billed as an opportunity to establish all of these wonderful connections and business opportunities. But that's not what I'm talking about here. Instead, I'm talking about events that people want to attend. Instead of a wine and cheese hour, host a wine tasting with a noted sommelier or a well-respected winery. That way, people can learn and sample exceptional wines while making connections. I love attending events with notable guest speakers. One featured a fighter pilot who had been tasked with flying over New York City on 9/11. You could have heard a pin drop in that room. Every one of us took something away from that talk, which made it far more successful than if we had just been standing around.

Simply taking the time to connect with a client on a personal level goes a long way toward building that rapport. If I know a client is a huge Rutgers basketball fan, I'll set an alert for the team. That way, the next time I talk to that person, I'll be able to connect with a simple, *Hey John, fantastic game on Saturday*, or I can email that person and commiserate with something like, *Wow, what a heartbreaking fourth quarter*. It's a point of contact that says I'm paying attention—and I care.

Generating as many of these points of contact as possible is key. That's one reason why Lewis & Llewellyn sends out a newsletter every six weeks. Admittedly, I rank newsletters just below e-cards on the list of thoughtful outreach; however, there are ways to make them worth your client's while. That means going beyond telling readers what your firm has been doing and, instead, providing them information they can really use. We generate confidence in our clients and potential clients by providing value.

For example, each month as part of our newsletter, we include a litigation tip of the month. Those tips are intended to be directly applicable for litigators, of course. But they also give other clients some insight into the work that we do, and they have the added benefit of demonstrating that we actually know what we're talking about (imagine, for instance, if your cardiologist offered a heart surgery tip of the month; probably, you'd feel better about having her open up your chest). The best compliment I can receive is when someone says our marketing department has really nailed a newsletter. Why? Because we don't *have* a marketing department. Instead, it's me and my team, literally agonizing over every single word in the newsletter to make sure we've made it pitch-perfect for the thousands of people who will receive it.

As important as it is to foster and care for our clients, it's equally important to acknowledge our internal teams. At Lewis & Llewellyn, we make it a point to express gratitude toward our team. Cash bonuses are fine, but they don't have an emotional impact. A personalized gift goes a long way toward saying that a person really matters.

For instance, an associate of ours is a huge pizza fan, so when he and his family relocated, we sent them gift cards for several of the top pizzerias in their new town. It didn't cost us much money, but it showed we took the time to learn what he really cares about—and to show that we really care about him.

A few years ago, we tried a big case that required us to travel and stay in a hotel. One of the lawyers on our team would wake up every morning and use the Peloton in the hotel gym. After we won the case, we sent her a Peloton of her own. Later, she told us it was one of the most thoughtful things anyone had ever done.

There's nothing unique about any of this to law firms, of course. The same concepts I've been outlining in this chapter could be applied to accounting firms or other types of companies. And that brings me to my larger point. As lawyers, we forget that we are ultimately building and running a business. We ignore the fact that, at the end of the day, we're salespeople selling a service. Yes, that service has to be top-notch. But if we don't take the time to sell that service, we're never going to have clients who need it.

Too many lawyers see the concept of selling as one with negative connotations: it brings to mind used car salespeople (who, you probably remember, are one of only two types of professionals listed below us in trustworthiness and likeability). I'd argue that not only should we ignore those connotations, but we should also embrace our roles as salespeople. As lawyers, we are problem solvers. Solving someone else's problem is why many of us chose this career. Of course, we should sell that service: it's important, it's needed, and it will make that person's life much, much better.

The reality of our profession is that it is always changing. You might have a thriving practice in one area, but then statute limitations change or the legislature caps damages, and suddenly the gravy train is over. We have to remain hungry and nimble. Becoming complacent about our clientele can be a death sentence in this dynamic field.

Empowering not just partners but every member of a firm to embrace this idea will only benefit the firm—and every member of its team. This is particularly true for young or junior attorneys there. In a well-functioning firm, there's a good chance they will work their way up to senior roles. Empowering them with a budget for gift giving encourages business development now that they can take with them in future years. And if you happen to be one of these junior lawyers, it's equally important that you think about the realities of our profession. As much as it may be ideal to imagine you'll stay with one firm for your entire career, the truth is that that's rarely the case. Having your own roster of committed clients gives you job security and the ability to transfer to another firm or even begin one of your own. Cultivating clients allows you to become your own advocate and ultimately puts you in control of your own destiny.

Just recently, I received a new case from a woman who serves as general counsel for a well-respected company. I've known her and her deputy professionally for some time, but we hadn't spoken in a decade. When the general counsel called to retain us, she told us the backstory: *My deputy and I were both independently thinking that we needed new litigation counsel,* she told me. *And we both said, what about Lewis & Llewellyn?* As it turned out, they'd been getting our monthly newsletters for years. We'd stayed in the front of their minds, quietly providing value. And so, when they became dissatisfied with their current counsel and the time came to change, they'd both independently chosen us. They'd seen our results; they'd seen how we live our philosophy and take care of both our clients and our team.

I like to joke that life is too short for anyone to need a litigator. But if someone does need to litigate, I want the one and only firm they think of to be ours. Keeping in constant, meaningful contact with our clients doesn't just help ensure that they'll call whenever they need us. It also builds us an exponential network of referrals that includes all of their contacts as well. Building rapport and relationships now means they'll be that much more likely to stick with your firm for years to come. Or, if I may say it, become a member of your cult.

NOTES

1   "The Alarming Alcoholism Rates for Lawyers," The Recovery Village, last updated May 26, 2022, https://www.therecoveryvillage.com/alcohol-abuse/alarming-alcoholism-rate-lawyers/.

2   Taylor Borden, "Judge Judy's Show Is Ending After 25 Years. Here's How One of the Highest-Paid Personalities in TV History Makes and Spends Her $440 Million Fortune," Business Insider, March 4, 2020, https://www.businessinsider.com/judge-judy-sheindlin-net-worth-how-she-made-her-money-2020-3.

3   "Honesty/Ethics in Professions," Gallup, accessed November 9, 2022, https://news.gallup.com/poll/1654/honesty-ethics-professions.aspx.

4   Center for Justice & Democracy, New York City, "McDonald's Hot Coffee Case – Read the Facts NOT the Fiction," Texas Trial Lawyers Association, accessed October 27, 2022, https://www.ttla.com/index.cfm?pg=McDonaldsCoffeeCaseFacts.

5   Dan Packel, "In a Stellar Year for the Global 200, Geography Was Paramount," Law.com, September 21, 2021, https://www.law.com/international-edition/2021/09/21/in-a-stellar-year-for-the-global-200-geography-was-paramount/; "GDP (Current US$)," The World Bank, accessed October 27, 2022, https://data.worldbank.org/indicator/NY.GDP.MKTP.CD.

6   ALM Staff, "Early Reports: The 2022 Am Law 200 Financials," Law.com, April 6, 2022, https://www.law.com/americanlawyer/2022/04/06/early-reports-the-2022-am-law-200-financials/.

7   Joe Patrice, "Big Takeaways from The Am Law 100 Profits per Equity Partner Ranking," Above the Law, April 27, 2022, https://abovethelaw.com/2022/04/big-takeaways-from-the-am-law-100-profits-per-equity-partner-ranking/.

8   Leigh Jones, "Lawyers Reveal True Depth of Mental Health Struggles," Law.
    com, February 19, 2020, https://www.law.com/international-edition/2020/02/19/
    lawyers-reveal-true-depth-of-the-mental-health-struggles-378-134739/.

9   Michael S. Webb, "Dissenting from Death: Preventing Lawyer Suicide," American Bar
    Association, November 24, 2021, https://www.americanbar.org/groups/senior_lawyers/
    publications/voice_of_experience/2021/voice-of-experien.

10 "Forbes Profile: Joe Jamail, Jr.," *Forbes*, accessed October 27, 2022, https://www.forbes.com/
    profile/joe-jamail-jr/?sh=5463ba3942e0.

11 John Spong, "The Greatest Lawyer Who Ever Lived," *Texas Monthly*, January 2015, https://www.
    texasmonthly.com/the-culture/the-greatest-lawyer-who-ever-lived/.

12 "Judge/Magistrate Salary in California," Salary.com, accessed October 27, 2022, https://www.
    salary.com/research/salary/benchmark/judge-magistrate-salary/ca.

13 Tony Hsieh, "How I Did It: Zappos's CEO on Going to Extremes for Customers,"
    Harvard Business Review, July–August 2010, https://hbr.org/2010/07/
    how-i-did-it-zapposs-ceo-on-going-to-extremes-for-customers.

14 "How Does Your Law Firm's NPS Stack Up?" Law Technology Today, April 12, 2019, https://www.
    lawtechnologytoday.org/2019/04/how-does-your-law-firms-nps-stack-up/#:~:text=The%20
    legal%20industry%20currently%20has,in%20the%2060's%20or%20higher.

15 David DiSalvo, "Study: Anger and Heart Attacks Strongly Linked," Harvard Medical School,
    June 9, 2013, https://hms.harvard.edu/news/study-anger-heart-attacks-strongly-linked.